The ABCs of XML

The ABCs of XML

The Librarian's Guide to the eXtensible Markup Language

by Norman Desmarais

New Technology Press
Houston

Library of Congress Cataloging-in-Publication Data

Desmarais, Norman.
The ABCs of XML : the librarian's guide to the extensible
markup language / by Norman Desmarais.
p. cm.
Includes bibliographical references.
ISBN 0-9675942-0-0 (paperback)
1. XML (Document markup language) I. Title.
QA76.76.H94 D48 2000
005.7'2--dc21

00-008051

New Technology Press is an imprint of New Technology Press, Inc.

New Technology Press, Inc.
PO Box 842411, Houston, TX 77284-2411
Telephone: 281-646-7700
Fax: 281-646-7702
http://www.newtechnologypress.com

Printed in the United States of America

To Cecile

The song is ended;
but the melody lingers on.

Irving Berlin

Contents

Introduction vii

Chapter 1 XML and SGML 1

Chapter 2 XML Document Structure 11

Chapter 3 Doing It With Style 31

Chapter 4 Pointing and Linking 56

Chapter 5 Processing XML Data 89

Chapter 6 Managing XML Documents 101

Chapter 7 XML and Its Potential for E-Commerce 114

Chapter 8 Getting Started 137

Bibliography 152

Glossary 158

Appendix 1 Library of Congress' SGML Format 175

Appendix 2 Bibliographic Record in XML Format 180

Appendix 3 USMARC Record Converted from XML 183

Appendix 4 XML Format for Bibliographic Data 186

Index 190

Introduction

The Internet has sometimes been described as a large library where all the books are scattered on the floor. That is because there is no overall structure governing the organization of the information content. To get an idea of how difficult it is to manage unstructured data, such as that on the Internet, we just have to consider a search for the word "prince" which will retrieve many more items than we want to examine. It would not be unusual to retrieve thousands or even millions of loosely related URLs on everything from the musician or Prince Edward Island to Prince Charles (or any one of many other princes) because search engines cannot distinguish between the various definitions of the word: a musician, a part of Canada, or a member of a royal family.

Many people have expended a lot of effort over the years to try to put some order into this chaos but with varying degrees of success. XML, the eXtensible Markup Language, promises to change all that. It is a new language approved by the World Wide Web Committee (W3C) on February 10, 1998, after about a year and a half of work. The W3C established the SGML Editorial Review Board in 1996 to develop what would become the XML standard. This board became the XML Working Group. Their goals in designing XML were to make it compatible with SGML, easily transferred over a network, capable of supporting a wide variety of applications, and easy to write programs which process XML documents. They also wanted to minimize the number of optional features in XML and to make XML documents human-legible, reasonably clear, easy to create, and consistently processed by the receiver. Jon Bosak, the co-editor of the XML language, made a personal draft of a projected style section for the XML specification publicly available on the Internet in May, 1997. At the time, the XML specification was split into three parts, one for the language, one for style, and one for linking. Some of these parts have been further subdivided, as we'll see in the chapters discussing each part.

XML is actually more of a meta language, a language for describing languages. It is analogous to metadata which is data describing other data. For example, a catalog record such as the MARC record describes the item being catalogued. It is not the item itself. A meta language, such as XML, is broader than metadata in that it provides the syntax that allows users to create their own markup language and define their own vocabularies to meet specific application or industry needs (hence the "eXtensible" in XML). This capability lets users structure the data in an XML document any way they like and make the descriptions as specific as desired. XML can be used to describe data components, records, and other data structures -- even complex data structures.

This book attempts to provide an overview of XML and some of its possible applications in libraries. We begin with an overview of XML and its relationship to SGML and HTML. We examine the various components of the markup language. In the second chapter, we will discuss the structure of an XML document. This is not intended to be a tutorial on how to code documents but rather an explanation of the various components and how they can be used. Then, we will explore the different types of style sheets that offer various options for formatting and presenting XML documents for reading and processing. The fourth chapter covers XML's linking and pointing components. Hypertext links have made the World Wide Web the rich resource that it is. XML's linking and pointing components expand those capabilities even further.

One of the important advantages of XML is that it can be read by both humans and machines. The fifth chapter will discuss the processing of XML data and its import. As this data processing capability offers a new feature for the Web, XML's developers expect that electronic commerce (e-commerce) will be the "killer application" that will accelerate XML's adoption and catapult it into widespread use. We shall also consider both how to manage XML documents and how XML can facilitate document management. A glossary and bibliography round out our exploration.

As with all technological issues, XML is in a constant state of flux. To keep up to date on the status of the World Wide Web Committee's (W3C) work, point your Web browser to http://www.w3.org/TR. (The TR in the URL stands for Technical Reports.) There, you will find the latest versions of the W3C's documents. The W3C, which is made up of vendors and authors, is very democratic and does not require anything. Rather, it strongly suggests that vendors and authors abide by the principles of the Consortium.

Consequently, the W3C does not use the more common terms "specification" or "standard" to describe its output, even though many authors use these terms interchangeably. A completed document gets the designation of a "recommendation." It starts its life as a "note." The W3C uses the "note" designation for documents that have not yet reached even the working draft stage. This type of document is a dated, public record of an idea, comment, or document. It does not represent any commitment by the W3C to pursue work related to the Note. When a note gets accepted for review, a sub-committee of the W3C begins to work on it; and the "note" designation changes to "WD" which tells us that it is now a working draft of a W3C recommendation.

A document can remain a working draft for a considerable amount of time as it undergoes review and modification. This means that it is subject to change and revision at any time and does not imply consensus by a group or the W3C. As standards bodies and committees move more slowly than potential users, companies must either refrain from implementing a standard until it is complete or utilize it with the understanding that they may have to update their work periodically. Sometimes, companies will develop work-arounds until the specifications are complete. These work-arounds often become competing proprietary standards and may even become de facto standards if they become widely accepted in the marketplace. Ideally, these companies would replace their work-arounds to conform to the accepted standards when they can be implemented with a greater degree of certainty. When a W3C group reaches a degree of consensus, it proposes the recommendation to the Director to the Advisory Committee for review. At this time, the document gets the designation "Proposed Recommendation."

When a working draft has gone through the formal review process to become what we call a specification and the W3C calls a recommendation, the "WD" changes to "REC" for recommendation. A Recommendation is work that represents consensus within the W3C and has the Director's stamp of approval. This means the W3C considers that the ideas or technology specified by a Recommendation are appropriate for widespread deployment and promote its mission. The URL also indicates the date of the current version of the document, indicating year, month, and date. At the time of this writing, many of the components of XML have been accepted as Recommendations. XML itself was accepted as a recommendations on February 10, 1998. The components which have become recommendation, along with their dates include:

- Document Object Model Level 1 -- October 1, 1998. Both levels 1 and 2 define a platform- and language-neutral interface that allows programs and scripts to dynamically access and update the content, structure, and style of documents
- Synchronized Multimedia Integration Language (SMIL) -- June 15, 1998
- Namespaces -- January 14, 1999
- Resource Description Framework -- March 3, 1999
- Associating Style Sheets with XML documents Version 1.0 -- June 29, 1999

Those documents still in the working draft stage include:

- XML Linking Language (Xlink) -- March 3,1998
- XML Pointer Language (XPointer) -- July 9, 1999
- Document Object Model Level 2 -- March 4, 1999
- Extensible Stylesheet Language (XSL) -- April 21, 1999
- XML Path Language (Xpath) – Aug. 13,1999
- XML Signature Requirements – Aug. 20, 1999
- XSL Transformations (XSLT) – Aug. 13, 1999
- XML Schema Part 1: Structures -- May 6, 1999. This part proposes facilities for describing the structure and constraining the contents of XML 1.0 documents.
- XML Schema Part 2: Datatypes -- May 6, 1999. This part specifies a language for defining data types to be used in XML Schemas and, possibly, elsewhere.

In practice, the W3C pronouncements are implemented with little deviation, allowing people to refer to them in more absolute terms, such as specifications and standards. When people do deviate from the recommendations, it's usually by adding features. The W3C's work serves as minimum requirements on which to build; but the Web community does not look kindly on "feature bloat."

Chapter 1

XML and SGML

Before we begin to discuss XML, the eXtensible Markup Language, we need to understand XML's relationship to its parent, SGML (Standard Generalized Markup Language). This study will be brief. Those who want more technical comparisons between XML and SGML should consult the Comparison of SGML and XML technical note at http://www.w3.org/TR/NOTE-sgml-xml. After a brief examination of this relationship and its implications, we consider the Document Type Definition (DTD) which both languages use. We shall consider alternatives to the DTD and tools to build them. We shall also discuss the concepts of validity and well-formedness which determine whether or not an XML processor will be able to understand the document. We shall then explore some of the applications that use XML which are being developed for libraries.

XML is a subset of SGML (ISO 8879:1986 as amended and corrected). Initially conceived for use on the World Wide Web, XML can be used for any type of electronic publication. While SGML is a text processing standard that describes how a document should be laid out and structured, XML is a dialect of SGML that describes the information content of a document.

SGML really didn't catch on very well because it is too complicated, requiring a steep learning curve that corresponds to high costs. People were also reluctant to incur the expenses of hiring a consultant to implement and manage SGML. Instead, they focused on using the HyperText Markup Language (HTML) which, in its pure form, is an application of SGML with a Document Type Definition

(DTD). But HTML, as it is used in practice, is mostly presentation oriented. It defines how information is displayed, such as the color or font size of a word. It doesn't say anything about the actual meaning of the word. XML, on the other hand, has nothing to do with display. It only describes information.

HTML has a fixed set of tags; but XML lets users define their own tags, making it much more flexible and vendor independent. In other words, users can create XML documents in one application and use them in another without requiring a conversion. Because XML accommodates a virtually unlimited number of tags, it can describe the information content of a document more precisely. An XML tag can describe the meaning of any word or term, such as a person's name, a product name, date, or whatever.

For example, searching for the term "pocketbook" in HTML could retrieve items dealing with a purse, a billfold or wallet, or a small book because there has been no way to identify the sense or the meaning of the search term. With XML, developers can tag data to distinguish the different meanings of a word such as "bill" to identify a personal name, a bird's beak, a charge, a paper currency, or a proposed law -- something which is impossible with HTML.

This is particularly important for numbers which have no inherent meaning in themselves but derive their meaning from the context. While 1000 might be a good price, in dollars, to pay for a new state-of-the-art laptop computer, it would be a very bad average number of days to wait for delivery of purchases. The tag that puts the number in context and gives it meaning becomes critical. The tags also have associations or structure that permit finding, manipulating, acting on, and interacting with the data much more easily.

XML Processor

XML was designed to be easy to implement and to work with both SGML and HTML. It is intended to work in such a way that the Web will be able to handle generic SGML in much the same way that is now possible with HTML. XML describes the information content of documents, called XML documents. It also describes, to some degree, how computer programs will process those documents. XML uses a software module called an XML processor or parser to read XML documents and to provide access to their content and structure. The XML processor interfaces with an application, such as a web browser or word processor, which allows further manipulation of the document. XML permits handling data in a variety of formats and from a variety of sources without costly programming or time delays of data conversion.

Data Type Definition and Alternatives

Those familiar with SGML know that SGML documents use a Document Type Definition (DTD) to specify the structure of a document. The acronym is sometimes referred to as a Document Type Declaration or as a Data Type Definition. Some people prefer the latter term because it is broader and more all-encompassing. Sometimes, the term XML-Data Schema is used to avoid any confusion. The XML DTDs or XML Data Schemas can use as data formats the structural relationships between elements and the XML vocabularies which identify those elements used in particular data formats. Only "valid" (more on this later) XML data require a DTD.

The DTD is only needed at the time of document creation and not for browsing. It consists of two parts: a formal part for the computer to understand the structure of the information and an informal part for a person to identify what the information is or what it means. It is not envisioned that people will write their own DTDs from scratch but rather use tools like Microstar Software Ltd.'s Near & Far Designer which is a visual modeling tool for building SGML and XML structures that can also convert DTD formats.

The XML Data Schema performs the function of a DTD and specifies the nature of the various elements in a document. It consists of two parts, still in working draft mode. XML Schema: Structures defines the language of an XML document and proposes facilities for describing the structure and constraining the contents of XML documents. The schema language provides a superset of the capabilities found in XML 1.0 document type definitions. XML Schema Part 2: Datatypes specifies a language for defining datatypes to be used in XML Schemas and, possibly, elsewhere. XML Schemas, then, will probably serve as application-specific DTDs, such as for particular types of business or industry, such as libraries, museums, and so on. They will specify the vocabulary and formalize the syntax for applications, provided the respective organizations can come to agreement. Schemas will use a schema document in standard XML syntax rather than a separate DTD syntax.

MARC

The MARC format could easily serve as the XML Data Schema for library applications (1), as it contains all the information needed by librarians and anybody working in the book industry. In fact, MARC has been referred to as the “grand-daddy of all DTDs.” Already about 30 years old, the MARC format is beginning to show its age. The Library of Congress began, in 1995, to consider the feasibility of using SGML to encode USMARC records. It subsequently released MARC DTDs that define USMARC data in SGML format (Appendix 1). Early in 1998, the library announced software to convert between USMARC and SGML (see: http://www.loc.gov/marc/#marcdtd for details.) The objective is to make machine-readable bibliographic data more open and interchangeable in the Internet environment. It would be relatively easy to use or convert SGML into XML so Web pages will not just display the layout, but also be able to interpret the semantic structure of its content. Bibliographic records can be interchanged between XML and MARC without any data loss (see Appendix 2 and 3); and many of the problems associated with the MARC format, including foreign characters, romanization, and authority control, become insignificant. See Appendix 4.

Catalog librarians might want to distinguish between personal authors, joint authors, corporate authors, etc. and title proper, collective title, uniform title, etc., while book dealers putting together a catalog or students preparing a bibliography are just interested in author and title information without any finer distinctions.

The MARC format as an XML Data Schema could serve all of these functions by describing the syntax for this purpose or for exporting information about books, titles, and authors to a relational or object-relational database where another XML Data Schema could describe row types and key relationships. XML Data Schemas can provide a common vocabulary for ideas which overlap between syntactic, database, and conceptual schemas making all features usable together as appropriate.

Using the MARC format as an XML Data Schema can also serve to specify books by, rather than about, Charles Darwin, for example. Current engines for searching the Web cannot make this distinction because the document structures do not make it. So they mix both types of books together. Likewise, if a researcher wants to distinguish Darwin's manuscripts from printed editions or facsimile editions, this too is difficult.

Because every database describes its data differently, a search engine cannot understand the various schemas which describe how each database is built. XML could easily categorize books in a standard way, using the MARC format, so that agents could search bookstore sites by author, title, ISBN, or other criteria in a consistent way, much like Z39.50 engines do for library catalogs. Unlike with Z39.50, however, XML would not require re-mapping of the data. A searcher could identify only stores that stock a particular title, for example, instead of retrieving all the places which cite or mention it. One could also limit the search only to articles that review that book.

Building DTDs

Logos Research Systems, Inc. developed a small utility that "round-trips" MARC records to "well-formed" XML and back. This utility, called MARCXML, uses a very simple XML format that isn't designed to contain any knowledge of the MARC records other than the basic structure. In other words, because it only encodes the raw structure of the file, it has no built-in understanding of USMARC or any other MARC format and cannot detect improper use of tags during an XML to MARC conversion. It doesn't know what's allowed to repeat, what's obsolete, etc. There is a small DTD; but the converter doesn't require it to rebuild the record. Nor does it perform character set conversions. The resulting XML file can be viewed in a browser or edited in a word processor and then recompiled back into a structurally valid MARC record. The XML parser is built into the converter; so the whole thing runs as one small program. A demonstration of the conversion in both directions can be run from Logos Research Systems's web site at http://www.logos.com/marc. The company also has a free MARCType Parser which parses USMARC records into an annotated human-readable document online.

The Graphical Communication Association Research Institute and the Data Interchange Standards Association plan to build libraries of Document Type Definitions, Java applets, template scripts, forms, and object definitions to allow businesses to process the components of XML messages.

Microsoft Corp. and IBM have also developed Document Content Descriptions (DCD), written entirely in XML, to replace DTDs. They submitted the proposal to the World Wide Web Consortium (W3C) on July 31, 1998. The W3C will form a working group to consider it and to flesh out the protocol (see www.w3.org/TR/NOTE-dcd). DCDs intend to provide similar functionality to DTDs; but they won't require users to learn XML and a DTD protocol. They will also support other XML-related components such as:

> Resource Description Framework (RDF) which provides an infrastructure to support metadata (data about data) across Web-based activities and can be used to describe the content and content relationships available at a particular Web site, page, or digital library.
>
> XML-Schema which proposes facilities for describing the structure and constraining the contents of XML documents.

XML Namespaces which qualifies tag names used in XML documents by associating them with their source and provides a simple method for qualifying certain names used in XML documents by associating them with namespaces.

XPointer (XML Pointer Language) which supports addressing into the internal structure of XML documents. This allows going directly to a specific section, paragraph, table, or other element contained in a document instead of referencing the document as a whole.

"Valid" and "Well-Formed" XML

We have already used the terms valid and well-formed; but we have not yet mentioned what they mean. Consistency is an important part of XML implementation. Each type of industry will have to come to some agreement on the metatags its members will use and develop appropriate DTDs for use by its members. If we are to be able to compare book prices, for example, booksellers will need to use the same tags. Using synonymous terms like price, list price, selling price, retail price, wholesale price, discount price, or charge to describe the same entity will only perpetuate the confusion and hinder data sharing. In the chaotic world of the Web, it may be difficult to achieve that level of agreement.

In the world of XML and SGML, the DTD specifies the tags and their meanings so applications can work with and manipulate the data. Documents that make use of internal or external Data Type Definition files are known as "valid" XML and require an XML parser to check incoming data against the rules defined in the DTD to verify that the data were structured correctly.

A developer usually decides which parser to integrate into an application or builds one from scratch; so an end-user has no control over which parser to use. There are two kinds of parsers: validating and non-validating. A validating parser “validates” documents by ensuring that they conform to the DTDs specified within them. A non-validating parser only checks that the document has a sound logical structure and syntax ("well formed"). Internet Explorer 4 uses a non-validating parser; but IE5 beta-1 uses a validating parser. Netscape Navigator 5.0 will use a non-validating parser written in C which is faster and more efficient than a Java parser.

Parsers must know what the elements mean and how to process them. (We’ll discuss elements in more detail in the next chapter.) XML allows developers to describe element names in a recognizable manner to avoid conflicts between elements with the same name. For example, some applications may have valid reasons for distinguishing between list price, retail price, wholesale price, and discount price, depending on a company's business rules and markets. Using different tags just to be different, however, will only lead to confusion. The W3C is considering a proposal to make every element name subordinate to a Uniform Resource Identifier (URI) to ensure that names remain unambiguous even if chosen by multiple authors.

The creators of the XML format admit that it is primarily intended to meet the requirements of large-scale Web content providers. However, valid XML files can be used outside the Web, such as in an SGML environment, for electronic publishing or as a means to produce print products.

Data sent without a DTD is known as "well-formed." That data can be used implicitly to describe itself. XML encoded data is self-describing and can also be used to model and deliver structured data without any reference to documents. This allows XML's open and flexible format to exchange or transfer information. It also makes XML extremely powerful, as it can be used for any type of information, such as articles, chapters, books, maps, weather forecasts, invoices, purchase orders, order forms, and so on.

XML only requires data to be "well-formed." In other words, its logical structure must appear sound. Its elements must be properly nested with all opening tags subsequently closed. Otherwise, browsers will look for a closing tag until it times out, resulting in slower speed of delivery to end-users.

Applications

XML will be particularly useful for enabling a Web client to interact with two or more sources of data at the same time. These sources may have different formats or require access through dissimilar interfaces. If they have common tags giving meaning to the data attributes, XML applications will be able to work with them. Search engines will be able to understand and use contextual information when performing a full-text search, producing more relevant results. They will also be able to work across incompatible hardware and software platforms and with incompatible protocols.

OCLC's SiteSearch, for example, can load XML records, build interfaces, and permit powerful cross database searching by using XML templates. The template allows extracting information from a database of records stored in XML format. It can also map MARC records to XML for editing and creation of new records. That information can then be used as a form to populate another record, creating a populated template which can then be displayed in HTML, XML, or another format.

While reading an article, for example, a student can consult a footnote, get an abstract of a reference, verify whether the local library or a remote library has the item, or prepare a purchase requisition – all without leaving one's place in the article. Another example would be the ability to go from a citation in an index or bibliography to the full text of the cited work.

Endeavor Corp. is working on a product called ENCompass which it expects to introduce in the year 2000. It will support various DTDs, such as Dublin Core for digital content, Text Encoding Initiative (TEI) for full text content, and Encoded Archival Description (EAD) for archival material. It will also allow searching across disparate databases with different file structures, terminology, etc. to provide an integrated display of resources regardless of whether they're described in MARC, TEI, EAD, or Dublin Core.

The product will allow users to go from a catalog record citation, a reference or footnote, or an abstract or bibliographic citation to the full text from different aggregators. One could start from a catalog record or a citation to look up an ISBN in *Books in Print* to get ordering information, availability, and pricing. One could also consult an author biography in *Who's Who* or search related items in other databases.

ExLibris is developing its Aleph search engine which recognizes XML encoding. It is also working on the ability to index based on XML encoding. It plans to support XSL, the eXtensible Stylesheet Language (see chapter 3), when the draft becomes finalized.

Many library system vendors are experimenting with XML applications. Data Research Associates, for example, is experimenting with passing XML-encoded patron data to OCLC. XML may bring more uniformity to the different ways vendors authenticate clients.

XML can take the strain off Web sites by moving much of the processing load from the Web server to the Web client where a Java applet downloaded to the user's PC, for example, may do the processing. Dynamic HTML also uses this approach; but an applet can do more with XML-tagged content because the data possess much more meaning. This will have a dramatic impact on Electronic Data Interchange (EDI) and electronic commerce which we'll discuss further in chapter 7.

A Web client can interact with multiple views of the same data, unlike in the HTML world where each different view requires a trip back to the server for re-presentation. An XML client can sort, filter, and manipulate data locally, making it much easier to customize a presentation to the needs of the person using the data. A catalog librarian can have one view of the data; a library patron can have another; accounts payable can have yet another. By supporting a greater granularity of information, XML allows individuals to extract relevant information from several sources and reassemble it into any format (data re-purposing).

Intelligent Web agents can also be programmed to find and deliver information to meet profiles tailored to each individual. Those profiles could be customized in terms of both content and presentation. After retrieving the information, the browser could use the tags to omit irrelevant portions and display only those portions of a document most likely to interest the reader. This could reduce information overload and accelerate learning. This capability would also allow individuals to create "custom" documents or reports with the most recent information formatted and delivered any way they want it.

NICEM (National Information Center for Educational Media) has converted its database from a simple relational database management system to an XML-based intranet system in an effort to provide higher-quality new records. By storing the bibliographic records as XML documents, the data are useable by any system that meets standardized criteria.

NICEM has also developed a machine-aided indexing (MAI) application to accompany the new system. The MAI program utilizes the NICEM thesaurus of 4300 subject terms along with 6000 syntax rules written by NICEM editors. It uses natural language processing to read the bibliographic record and then suggest subject terms to the editor. This process takes only seconds and provides the editor with terms he or she can decide to use or ignore. The editor can also select subject terms from the thesaurus to include in the record. MAI provides for faster indexing and promotes consistency in indexing from editor to editor. XML could also be used to discover new relationships between data, whether in searching or display.

The Association of American Publishers (AAP) and John Wiley & Sons have collaborated on establishing a clearinghouse for metadata in an attempt to establish standardized systems for managing digital book and journal publishing. The Metadata Information Clearing House (Interactive) – MICI -- is an online interactive database that will allow publishers to input comments, questions, and descriptive information about their metadata procedures. It will also let users know who's working on what. It will also allow publishers to identify and locate digital content and to establish links and relationships among different kinds of content..

The MICI project is expected to eventually ensure more comprehensive and accurate search engine results, content reuse, and analysis of customer activity. It will probably also incorporate the Digital Object Identifier (DOI). More information on MICI can be obtained from the AAP Web site (http://www.publishers.org/mici.htm) or from John Wiley's site (http://wileynpt.com/mici).

The AAP also surveys the systems used by publishers to process and transmit online bibliographic and descriptive content to online retailers. This includes such basic information as book jacket images, catalog entries, and author background.

Outlook

XML is not a single, fixed format like HTML, nor is it a replacement for HTML. XML is a metalanguage that lets users design their own markup languages to meet specific application or industry needs. It provides a standard way for describing and exchanging data regardless of its nature, how the sending system stored it, or how the receiving system will use it.

HTML will continue in use for the foreseeable future because of the cost and labor to tag existing documents. The change will be evolutionary; but its impact will be revolutionary. Versions of HTML subsequent to HTML 4.0 will use XML syntax and support XML tags. As Web pages get updated and modified, the code will gradually get converted to XML, producing a richer, more relevant, and better organized Web.

In this chapter, we examined XML's relationship to its parent, SGML and some of its implications. We looked at the Document Type Definition (DTD), alternatives to it, and tools to build DTDs. We discussed the related concepts of validity and well-formedness and explored some library applications that use XML. Now that we have a foundation, we can turn our attention to the structure of an XML document.

Notes

1. Lam, K. T. Moving from MARC to XML. http://home.ust.hk/~lblkt/xml/marc2xml.html

Chapter 2

XML Document Structure

One of the principles underlying XML is that the content of the documents be accessible to and readable by both humans and machines (computer software). Consequently, documents in XML format will contain a mixture of text and markup (tags) which organize and identify the components of a document. Word processors, desktop publishing systems, and authoring tools usually have a WYSIWYG (What You See Is What You Get) interface that hides the markup codes from the author; but they are there nonetheless, stored in a way that is more efficient for machine processing.

In this chapter, we begin with an overview of XML tags which enclose the vocabulary used by XML documents. Every document has both a logical and physical structure. The logical structure governs the conceptual organization and the underlying logic of a document. The physical structure determines how the various parts are stored and arranged. An XML document's logical structure is governed by elements defined in the XML declaration. We shall study the elements and how they work. We shall then discuss the various parts of the XML declaration, the element content model, and the attributes that modify and further specify the elements.

We shall then proceed to the physical structure defined and governed by the entities. We shall consider the rules that regulate their use. We shall then examine the different types of entities and how they work. Just as elements have attributes to modify them and to provide further specifications, entities have notations which are particularly useful for processing non-textual material. The physical and logical structures of an XML document do not have to correspond; but they do have to be properly nested. Elements must begin and end in the same entity. Comments, processing instructions, character references, and entity references must all be contained entirely within the same entity.

Tags Create the Markup

An XML document can be considered as a folder that contains other folders or as an envelope that contains other envelopes. XML tags specify the beginning and end of each envelope. Just as HTML and SGML tags, XML tags begin with a left angle bracket (<) and end with a right angle bracket (>) as in the following example:

<title>The Old Man and the Sea</title>

XML tags always occur in pairs and are usually referred to in the singular, as the title tag above, with the end tag implied. The tag constitutes the markup; and whatever occurs between the start and end tags is the content. Some tags, like the
 (line break) tag in HTML, do not have any content. The tag itself specifies the function it performs. These tags would usually be represented as <br> and </br>. However, XML allows abbreviating the start and end tags of an empty tag to begin with a left angle bracket and end with a slash and a right angle bracket, such as <br/>. An empty tag is typically used as a place holder for an image, for example.

Just as in an algebraic formula, all tags must be perfectly nested within one another. HTML would allow the following expression:

<head><title>The Old Man and the Sea</head></title>

XML would not. To be acceptable in XML, the closing </head> and </title> tags would need to be reversed.

Tags are not case-sensitive in HTML; but they are in XML. Consequently, <title>, <Title>, <TITLE>, and <tITle> all represent different things to the XML processor. Also, the end tag must match exactly the name that appears in the start tag. Case sensitivity allows defining different elements with the same name; but this is not usually advisable as it would be too easy for authors to select the wrong element. In addition, certain keywords, especially in the DTD itself, must always be capitalized.

Another difference between HTML and XML is the way they handle white space, anything that separates words or characters from one another (including punctuation). HTML treats all white space the same, collapsing every occurrence of it into a single space. This includes multiple spaces, carriage returns and line feeds, as well as tabs and indentations. XML assumes all white space to be significant and maintains it. However, XML browsers may still collapse the white space into a single space.

Typesetting languages use a series of tags, each with a pre-defined purpose to change the appearance of the text or its location on the page. Some, such as in desktop publishing systems, group several instructions as a macro. For example, a macro called "title" could specify that the text governed by it should appear in bold, italic, Caxton typeface, 20 point font size, and centered.

Elements Define the Logical Structure

The function of the markup in an XML document is to describe its storage and logical structure and to associate attribute-value pairs with its logical structures. XML markup builds on the concept of macro-based typesetting languages. Here, the tags name the object rather than specify a particular presentation style. By mapping element tags to conventional typesetting tags, such as with a style sheet, one can change the output style at any time without having to re-tag the text. The start and end tags together with their contents constitute the elements of an XML document and define its logical structure. The terms tag and element are often used interchangeably.

Element names are always tokens, meaning that a name is just a sign or symbol of something else. Computer-processed text requires that a token appear as a single "word" with no spaces; so descriptive tags need to be condensed in some form to make them understandable to both humans and computers. This can sometimes present problems designating particular tags.

One solution would be to capitalize each component "word" or all of them but the first. A patron address tag, for example, could appear as <patronAddress> or <PatronAddress>. Another solution would replace the space with some other legal but non-alphabetic character such as a punctuation mark. In this case, the format would look like:

<patron_address>, <patron-address>, or <patron.address>.

XML elements are the basic building blocks of the markup in an XML document. They can contain more elements as long as all the elements are properly nested or embedded. For example, a book contains several chapters, each with several sections and subsections. An author must conclude a section before proceeding to the following section or chapter. We saw, in the previous chapter, that when an XML document's elements are properly enclosed, it is called a well-formed document.

Some elements can be repeated to contain themselves directly or indirectly. An optional DTD pre-defines which elements are allowed within other elements and contains the rules for each element allowed within a specific class of documents. In lieu of a DTD, an XML document may contain instructions to the XML processor within markup declarations in the prolog, at the beginning of the document.

An XML document does not have to include a prolog; but it can provide information to an application program, such as a browser, about what to display and how to display it. It can also serve to explain the document's purpose and scope for human readers or contain comments.

The prolog can consist of four elements: the XML declaration, comments, processing instructions and the document type declaration. The simplest form of the prolog contains only the XML declaration.

XML Declaration

The XML declaration may contain three pieces of information: the version of XML, the character set, and whether on not the browser needs to access an external DTD to interpret the document's content.

The XML declaration uses the tags for processing instructions (PI) rather than those for a markup declaration which begin with the left angle bracket and exclamation point (<!) and end with the right angle bracket (>). Hence, the XML declaration opens with <? and closes with ?>. The PIs tell the program processing the content that it may need to take some particular action. In the example below, it tells the program, the browser, that the material that follows is an XML document that conforms to version 1.0 of the XML specification.

If the browser is intelligent enough, it will understand the PI and allow processing only according to the rules of that XML version. It will not allow any markup that's only acceptable by a later version or by any HTML version. The XML specification currently exists only in version 1. The fact that this statement appears in the prolog assumes that it will eventually undergo several revisions.

The prolog also may include either or both an encoding declaration and a standalone document declaration, depending on how complete one wants to make the XML declaration. The encoding declaration tells the browser what character set it needs to be able to process the document. This allows for using Chinese, Japanese, Korean, Arabic, or other scripts. (See appendices 2, 3, 4.)

The standalone document declaration tells the XML processor whether or not the document and its rules are completely self-contained. It takes yes/no values to specify whether or not the DTD is located in some other file. Thus, the full XML declaration:

```
<?xml version=1.0"
encoding="UTF-8"
standalone="yes"?>
```

tells the browser or human reader that the document is an XML document conforming to the XML specification version 1.0, that it uses the default UTF-8 encoding scheme for the standard ASCII character set, and that it contains all the markup and the document structure.

Comments

The comments section lets one include a description of a section of code, notes on how to use it, etc. much like the comments included in program code in other languages. It can serve as a Post-It® note to oneself to refresh one's memory months after creation when one has forgotten what a particular section of code was meant to accomplish. Comments need not be restricted to the prolog. They can occur anywhere in the document and can go on for several lines. They use the same delimiters as HTML comments: <!-- and –> and can contain anything except a pair of adjacent hyphens that signal the end of the comment. A comment can contain special symbols and XML components that would otherwise be reserved for XML processing, such as the angle brackets.

Processing Instructions

We've already seen that the XML declaration is an example of a processing instruction. PIs are always enclosed in opening <? and closing ?> delimiters. The content of a PI depends on the nature of the software which is expected to process certain types of content not covered by the XML conventions (specified as a keyword and known as the target) or to perform some non-XML function. For example, the instruction

```
<?realaudio version="5.0" frequency="5.5kHz" bitrate="16Kbps"?>
```

identifies the properties of any Real Audio files it may encounter and tells the processor how to handle them.

Document Type Declaration

The document type declaration is XML's mechanism to define the logical structure and to support the use of predefined storage units. In other words, it specifies the markup language that is used and tells the processing software which document type definition to use to understand the document.

Markup declarations begin with the left angle bracket and exclamation point (<!) and end with the right angle bracket (>). Sometimes, markup declarations group a number of other declarations. When this occurs, a subset structure identifies the embedded declarations by enclosing them in square brackets. The actual tags used to mark the boundaries between elements will vary from one XML application to another.

There are various kinds of markup declarations. A keyword, without any intervening spaces, at the beginning of the declaration identifies a specific declaration type. These specific types of declarations include DOCTYPE, CDATA, ENTITY, NOTATION, ELEMENT, ATTLIST, IGNORE, and INCLUDE.

The Document Type Declaration (DOCTYPE), if used, must appear near the top of the document. In its simplest form, the document type declaration identifies the name of the document element it precedes. More complex variants can serve to hold entity definitions or the DTD. The name is the only element required in this declaration and generally consists of just a label for the document type.

The syntax of a document type declaration is:

```
<!DOCTYPE name externalDTDpointer internalDTDsubset>
```

The externalDTDpointer identifies where to locate the markup rules to which the document conforms. The pointer consists of the keyword SYSTEM followed by the Uniform Resource Identifier (URI) that indicates the location of the DTD. The URI is identical in appearance and function to a Uniform Resource Locator (URL) for all practical purposes. These elements are referred to as the system ID.

The internalDTDsubset replaces or supplements an external DTD. It can contain anything that an external DTD can, and takes precedence over an external DTD in the event that a markup element is defined in both an external and an internal DTD. Internal DTD information is contained in square brackets to set it off from the rest of the doctype declaration. A very simple example showing all these elements for the address of a library patron would look something like:

<!DOCTYPE PatronRecord SYSTEM "http://www.library.edu/opac/patron.dtd" [!ELEMENT address ANY>]>

The Element Content Model

Besides identifying the element, the statement that names the element (its element type declaration) specifies the content of that element – its content model. An element's content model lets one specify precisely which elements are allowed inside an element, how often they appear, and in what order. It defines a template into which the content of all occurrences of the element will fit. This can consist of an element name or two or more element names grouped and sub-grouped. Each element may have various modifiers applied to it. The content model defines whether or not an element is required and whether or not it can be repeated. It also specifies the content type. Instead of a content model, the content specification could also be one of the keywords ANY or EMPTY.

A valid XML document requires that each element in the document have content that matches the content type statement. Because element types are always a single name, one must use a separate declaration for each element to declare more than one element type with the same content specification. For example:

```
<!ELEMENT uniformtitle (para+)>
<!ELEMENT title (para+)>
<!ELEMENT subtitle (para+)>
```

Defining a content model as a parameter entity, allows making changes in a single place. Parameter entities are entities that are used to define common or frequently-used parts of DTD code. We'll discuss parameter entities in more detail later.

If the content specification uses the keyword ANY, it specifies that the character data or elements may appear in any order. A content model may designate a particular element as EMPTY. This does not mean that the element is actually empty but that it requires no start and stop tag pairs. If they appear in the document, there is nothing between them. Using the EMPTY keyword specifies that the element may never have any content.

The content model does not define how many times an element may occur in the declaration of that element. It defines the occurrences in the content model of the containing element. This allows an element to occur several times depending on the context in which it appears. For example, an element defined as author might occur once and still cover several joint authors.

Groups of Elements

One can arrange elements into groups and specify container elements. Parentheses group different parts of the content model to allow one to declare that different types of content occur a different number of times in that content model. The simplest form of the element content model consists of a list of possible elements enclosed in parentheses and separated by commas, such as:

```
<!ELEMENT responsibility (author, editor, compiler, translator, illustrator)>
```

This statement would mean that all five functions must occur in the responsibility element and each may only occur once. This evidently will not suffice to describe areas of responsibility for a book as not all these functions occur in every work and some may occur more than once.

A vertical bar or pipe character (|) acts as a Boolean OR operator giving a choice of responsibilities. Even so, only one element can be selected, no matter how long the list of alternatives is. Grouping the element content into model groups combines content sequence and choice.

Unless specified, an element or group of elements must appear just once. An element occurrence indicator specifies how often an element or group of elements may appear. The ? character indicates that the element or group of elements may be omitted or may occur just once. The * character indicates that an element or group of elements may be omitted or may occur zero or more times. The + character indicates that an element or group of elements must appear at least once and may occur one or more times.

The following example:

```
<!ELEMENT responsibility ((author) | editor | compiler | translator |
illustrator)*)>
```

means that a title with mixed responsibility can contain any number of authors, editors, compilers, translators, or illustrators. The pipe character (|) acts as a Boolean OR operator; and the concluding asterisk indicates that the group as a whole can occur 0 or more times. If the asterisk were applied to each type of responsibility, it would mean that the statement of responsibility could include any number of authors or any number of editors, etc. which would produce entirely different results.

By identifying an element with the keyword #PCDATA (parsed character data) specifies that the element will contain only text. Here, an element name replaces the content type. The pound sign (#) prefix is called the reserved name indicator (RNI) and prevents one from confusing this keyword with a normal element name. It also makes it impossible to use it as a name. Parsed character data elements cannot contain any further markup. The end of the element start tag stops where the markup ends and "normal" text resumes.

XML content models only deal with the structure of an XML document and do not attempt to control the content. Consequently, an element can have no data content and still match a #PCDATA content model.

Attributes

Attributes provide metadata for elements and give designers more control over elements. They can specify formatting, security level, a revision status, and label elements for scripting. They can make elements respond to user actions and define default behaviors. Attributes are an excellent tool for passing extra information about an element to an automated processor, such as a parser, a browser, or a conversion tool. They are not a good place to actually store data, as a browser might render it only as a blank screen.

Elements can contain other elements; but attributes can contain only one value. This means that an author cannot nest information inside the attributes. Attributes should be used to store information that would be helpful for computers to process the information properly, rather than for human use.

All the attributes associated with a particular element are usually declared together in a single attribute list declaration. An attribute list declaration consists of one or more attribute declarations which are often put on separate lines for readability. Attribute list declarations may be used:

- To define the set of attributes pertaining to a given element type.
- To establish type constraints for these attributes.
- To provide default values for attributes.

Attribute declarations use a syntax similar to that for element declarations but tend to offer more precise definitions of the content they allow. The declaration begins with “<!ATTLIST” followed by the name of the element type and ends with the > character as the following syntax illustrates:

```
<!ATTLIST ElementName
    AttributeName Type Default
    (AttributeName Type Default...)>
```

The first value identifies the name of the element to which the attributes apply. The main body of the declaration contains a list of one or more attribute definitions, each of which has three parts:

1. The attribute name
2. The attribute data type
3. The default value

Names of attributes precede the value and they are separated by an equals sign (=). They must contain only letters, digits, periods, dashes, underscores, and colons, just as the names for elements and entities. XML accepts attributes enclosed in either single quotes or double quotes. Double quotes are more common; but single quotes are useful if an attribute includes a double quote. The attribute value is also enclosed in quotes so the parser will not misunderstand spaces as the end of a value when there are more attributes following.. To allow attribute values to contain both single and double quotes, the apostrophe or single-quote character (') may be represented as "'", and the double-quote character (") as """. Both the name and the value are case sensitive; so authors need to be careful to maintain consistency.

Attribute Types

String Attribute

The attribute type can be a string type, tokenized type, or enumerated type. The string attribute’s values consist of simple strings of characters. Here’s an example of a string type attribute declaration:

An attribute type declaration such as:

```
<!ATTLIST owner CDATA>
```

would be used like this:

<owner="Anytown Public Library">

Tokenized Attribute

Tokenized attributes are classified by their possible value(s). They include:

ID: which serves to identify the element. No two elements can have the same ID attribute value in the same document. An ID type declaration such as

<!ATTLIST book id ID>

would be used like

<book id="35125002851396"

Here, the number 35125002851396 is the book's barcode number.

IDREF: points to an ID and its value must match the value of an ID type attribute declared somewhere in the same document.

ENTITY: points to an external entity defined in the DTD. Its value consists of name characters corresponding to the name of the entity. This type of attribute would normally refer to things like graphics files and other unparsed data.

NMTOKEN: contains a token string consisting of any mixture of name characters.

These last three attributes also have plural forms (IDREFS, ENTITIES, NMTOKENS) to accommodate multiple values separated by spaces.

Enumerated Attributes

Enumerated attributes have values that are simply lists of possible values, each corresponding to a valid name token (NMTOKEN).

The final value of an attribute declaration is the default which specifies the action the XML processor should take when a particular tag does not contain a value. This value can be required (means that the attribute is required and should have been there), implied (allows the parser to ignore this attribute), fixed (a specified value), or default (a value that will be assumed if none is otherwise specified).

Reserved Attributes

XML reserves some attribute names for its own use. The prefix XML and any case variation (xml, xMl, etc.) is reserved to avoid conflict with user-defined attribute names. XML currently supports two special attributes that have this prefix: xml:lang and xml:space. The xml:lang attribute specifies the language used in the contents and attribute values of any element in an XML document. It can also be used with a sub-code to distinguish between variations of the same language, such as British English and American English. The xml:space attribute serves to tell the processing application that the element contains significant white space (space characters, line end codes, tabs, and indentations) that should be preserved. Unless specified, the application will consider this white space insignificant and collapse it.

Entities Define the Physical Structure

We have seen at the beginning of this chapter that the elements define an XML document's logical structure. Now we turn our attention to entities which make up an XML document's physical structure. A single XML document may consist of several separate files. This makes it easy to re-use the components within that document or within other documents. It also allows including non-XML data in the document. For example, an author may store each chapter of a book as separate files or may want to include an image in the text. Each unit of information is called an entity; and each entity has a name to identify it. The only entity that does not have an entity name is the document entity which contains the data that represents the entire document.

Every XML document starts with a single entity at the top level. The document's entity structure shows how the document's physical structure is laid out. It may consist of objects defined internally or stored on a file server, in a database, on the Internet, or anywhere else that is accessible.

A special tag, called an entity declaration, announces the entity 's existence and defines it. It appears at the top of the document entity and is similar to a document type declaration which contains the entity declarations which, in turn, define the entities before the first reference to them in the document. The entity declaration declares the existence of an entity, provides the entity with a name, and either holds the content of the entity or points to a file that holds it.

One may build a hierarchy of entities, beginning with the document entity. To use an entity, one inserts a reference to it within the text, much like a hyperlink. This reference identifies the desired entity; and its location in the text indicates where the content should appear. Just as with hyperlinks, a text may include several references to the same entity; but instead of just linking and jumping to the entity referred to, the content of the entity replaces each reference.

One would usually consider using an entity in one or more of the following circumstances:

> to avoid error-prone and time-consuming duplication when the same information is used in several places
>
> to represent the information differently by incompatible systems
>
> to avoid splitting a large document into smaller manageable units
>
> to use data that does not conform to the XML format

Rules of Use

Entities follow the same rules as other names in XML and are case sensitive. One can define the same entity more than once; but the XML processor will only acknowledge the first declaration. A document can contain any number of entity references (including none). Each reference "points to" a specific entity by referring to its name. The content of that entity then replaces the reference.

The text of an internal text entity is contained within single or double quotation marks as delimiters, as in the following example:

```
<!ENTITY XML "eXtensible Markup Language">
```

Double quotes are more common; but single quotes are useful if an attribute includes a double quote which would inadvertently be understood as the end of the entity.

Types of Entities

Excluding the XML document entity itself, there are three types of entities: character entities, general entities, and parameter entities. General entities can be further subdivided into internal entities and external entities. An entity is internal if its content is stored in the main document. It is external if its content resides in a separate file. External entities are further subdivided into parsed entities (containing character data which replaces the entity) and unparsed entities (resources whose contents may or may not be text, and, if text, may not be XML). A parameter entity is an entity that may only be referenced within markup declarations. It is used primarily by DTD designers to reduce their workload, to minimize the number of authoring errors, and to clarify the DTD structure. We shall not concern ourselves with it here.

Character Entity

A character entity is a special case of a general entity (discussed next). It refers to a specific character in the ISO/IEC 10646 character set. This type of entity allows easy access to and use of characters not directly accessible from available input devices. For example, to place a single special character in the XML document, such as a c with cedilla, one could use a statement like:

```
<!ENTITY ccedilla “&#231;”>
```

So, to enter the name François Mauriac in an XML document, one might render it thus,

```
Fran&ccedilla;ois Mauriac
```

or

```
Fran&#231;ois Mauriac
```

Here, the text of the entity begins with the usual & and ends with the ;. The pound sign (#) follows the ampersand which, in turn, is followed by a decimal or hexadecimal number that identifies the specified character. The decimal values, ranging from 0 to 255, represent the extended ASCII character set (ISO 8859/1) as used by Windows, Sun UNIX, and the Web. In this case, 231 refers to the c with cedilla. Decimal values ranging from 256 to 65535 represent additional characters from the larger Unicode/ISO 10646 character set. To enter a hexadecimal value requires an additional x character before the value: e.g.:

```
&#x3C;
```

which refers to the < character.

General Entity

A general entity is one that may be referred to within a document and is available to authors of documents. It functions like a shortcut for long text, boilerplate text, or a programmer's constants. It applies within the top-level element and in attribute values, such as:

<!ENTITY XML "eXtensible Markup Language">

An ampersand (&) designates the beginning of an entity in the document and a semicolon designates its end. These punctuation marks enclose the entity in the reference but do not appear in the entity declaration. Thus, a browser or other application would read the following example of an internal text entity:

The &XML; format includes entities.

and replace the entity with its definition thus:

The eXtensible Markup Language format includes entities.

This all occurs without the receiving application's awareness.

Every XML processor has some entity declarations built in. These are usually for characters that the XML processor understands as commands or instructions. Document authors must be aware of these characters and use appropriate character references to avoid confusing the XML processor which assumes every occurrence of these characters represents markup delimiters. These references are:

< for '<'
> for '>'
& for '&'
' for ' ' ' (in attribute values delimited by the same character)
" for ' " ' (in attribute values delimited by the same character)

To use an ampersand in the text of an entity, one would use the ampersand entity to avoid confusing the XML processor into thinking that the character represents the start delimiter of a general entity reference. For example, the following two entities

<!ENTITY XML "eXtensible Markup Language">
<!ENTITY CSS "Cascading Style Sheets">

can be combined with an ampersand

<title>&XML; & & CSS;</title>

to read:

eXtensible Markup Language & Cascading Style Sheets

Internal Entity

A general entity may be internal or external. An internal text entity is the simplest form of entity. It allows an author to pre-define any phrases or other text fragments that will be used repeatedly in the document. For example, a book about Ernest Hemingway will use his name often. One could avoid keying the whole name each time and also avoid possible misspellings by using an internal text entity called "name" to contain the entity's value, as in the following example:

<!ENTITY name "Ernest Hemingway">

External Entity

External entities have two ways to identify the location of their content: through a system identifier or through a public identifier. A system identifier indicates the location of an external text entity. This is accomplished by using the keyword SYSTEM followed by a quoted string that locates the file, as in:

<!ENTITY patron SYSTEM "/opac/patrons.xml"

A system identifier is reasonably straightforward and simply points to a file. References to external entities include at least a file name. They can specify either a relative path to a filename, such as ..\..\circ/patron.xml or an absolute path beginning at the root directory, such as h:/opac/circ/patron.xml . Using relative path names offers more flexibility because a collection of documents and directories can be moved to another system without editing the entity declarations. A relative link to a file in an embedded directory may appear as follows:

<!ENTITY patron SYSTEM "/opac/circ/patron.xml">

A system identifier can also be a Uniform Resource Identifier (URI) which is an enhancement of the Uniform Resource Locator (URL) system used for World Wide Web addresses. References to files on other systems must be preceded by the protocol and host name. The most common protocol used for file downloading is the HyperText Transfer Protocol (HTTP). So, to access the same file on Big University's server in the library subdirectory would look like this:

> <!ENTITY patron SYSTEM " **http://www.big.university.edu/library/** opac/circ/patron.xml">

A public identifier is another mechanism to locate an external entity. This method offers more flexibility because it provides more information on the content of the data file while not specifying directly the location and name of the file. The public identifier uses the keyword PUBLIC and can include such extra details as the language, the owner (or copyright holder), and the author.

A public identifier is always used in conjunction with a system identifier which it precedes. However, the SYSTEM keyword need not be included. The delimited system identifier itself is all that is required. The use of both public and system identifiers allows authors to access local resources when they are available. This is particularly useful for Web applications which should first compare a public identifier with locally stored entities. If the local system already contains the entity, it does not have to retrieve it from a remote Web server, saving time and bandwidth. If the public identifier does not specify any locally held entities or if the processor cannot locate them, then the system identifier locates the entity on the server and retrieves it.

Sometimes, an entity may consist of several paragraphs of text and may be too large to store conveniently in the document declaration. An entity might also need to draw on several documents for its content. It would be time consuming and error-prone to re-define an entity in each one. In these cases, one could store the text in a separate file and use an external text entity to access it. This would make it easy to edit the content separately from the document that refers to it.

Often, documents include non-textual information, such as drawings or photographs. Sometimes an author might want to incorporate other media types, such as sound and video, into documents. These types of materials are usually kept separate in binary data files which XML can reference. Because the binary data could confuse the XML processor, these entities cannot be merged-in to the document by the XML processor. Instead, the XML processor provides the name and location of the file, along with the notation it uses to the application. The application then uses this information either to process the data directly or to invoke another application to deal with it.

For example, a Web browser might have the capability to merge-in binary data to display it directly in a way that is totally transparent to the user. It may also invoke a plug-in or other application and prompt the user with a special icon to select and view the material. There is no limit to the size of the external file; and multiple documents can contain references to it. External text entities can also be used to group several internal entities, such as foreign character sets like Greek, Hebrew, Korean, Japanese, etc.

Parsed Data

An entity that contains XML data, regardless of whether it is stored internally or externally, is known as a parsed entity because it can be validated by an XML parser. A parsed entity's contents are referred to as its replacement text. This text is considered an integral part of the document. An external entity must have an external definition consisting of at least a system identifier which the parser will use to locate the text of the entity in a specified location outside of the document, such as:

```
<!ENTITY king.mov SYSTEM "file:///C:\ProgramFiles
      \QuickTime\QTinfo.exe">
```

Parsers read the internal DTD first and then the external DTD. If the internal DTD defines elements or entities, one cannot change those definitions in an external DTD.

The parser does not check the information; it just passes it to the processing application. If the processing application cannot understand it, as in the case of a Macintosh or UNIX application invoking a Windows executable file, the parser will continue its work without identifying any error. However, the processing application may produce an error; but it isn't an XML error.

Notations

Notations identify by name the format of unparsed entities, the format of elements which bear a notation attribute, or the application to which a processing instruction is addressed. An unparsed entity is a resource whose contents may or may not be text, and, if text, may not be XML. Each unparsed entity has an associated notation, identified by name. This unparsed data generally consists of binary files containing graphics, sound, or other multimedia elements. A notation identifies these elements and their format when they are declared as well as any helper application which will be required to process the data.

Defining notations in the DTD and including corresponding notation statements in the markup, then, makes it possible to incorporate multimedia into XML documents. Notation declarations provide a name for the notation, for use in entity and attribute-list declarations and in attribute specifications, and an external identifier for the notation which may allow an XML processor or its client application to locate a helper application capable of processing data in the given notation. A notation follows a syntax similar to that of the data attribute type declaration, such as:

```
<!NOTATION notation.name SYSTEM "program.url">
```

In the place of the notation.name and program.url variables, one identifies the particular media type and the location of the program that will handle the files of a particular media type. For example:

```
<!NOTATION mov SYSTEM "file:///C:\ProgramFiles
    \QuickTime\QTinfo.exe">
```

Now, whenever the XML application encounters a call for a QuickTime video (.mov) in an XML document, it will invoke QuickTime in the designated location to play the movie. This will only work if you know the name and location of the application that can handle a particular notation and if no one moves it. It is easier and more reliable to invoke an application residing on one's hard drive or network drive than it is to rely on the Internet.

Using a notation to specify external file viewers seems rather obsolete when most browsers support integrated features that handle a variety of graphics formats or can include a variety of plug-in tools to process non-integrated applications. The browser uses an internal table of Multipurpose Internet Mail Extension (MIME) types to maintain the association between media types and the plug-ins to run them. This corresponds somewhat to the notation names in an XML document.

Plug-in technology gives the user the appearance of a single unified Web page with the multimedia objects inside the browser window, even though different programs may control different portions of the window. Native XML browsers aren't quite that sophisticated yet; so the notation mechanism will probably still be useful to specify external processing, such as a link to a Java applet.

Authors can also use an existing SGML facility and a public identifier to handle multimedia. There are a lot of registered public identifiers for notations; so authors can easily use SGML declarations in XML documents. However, the SGML public identifiers have to be combined with system identifiers to do so. For example:

```
<!NOTATION GIF89a PUBLIC "-//CompuServe//NOTATION
        Graphics Interchange Format 89a//EN"
            "C:\ProgramFiles\ACDSee32\ACDSee32.exe">
```

This statement uses a system identifier; but it doesn't require the SYSTEM keyword.

One can also use the notation in one of the attribute declarations for an element by using the NOTATION keyword as in:

```
<!ELEMENT IMG EMPTY >
<!ATTLIST IMG
src %URL#REQUIRED
altCDATA#IMPLIED
typeNOTATION(GIF | JPEG | BMP) "GIF" >
```

In summary, notation declarations can be used in combination with processing instructions to handle nontextual information within a document. The notation declaration identifies the kind of information for the processor. The processing instruction tells it how to handle that information. Attributes can further specify whether an element needs its own window or should be presented in-line (along with the text and other material). While in-line presentation could make it easier to integrate XML with other applications, it will require the development of an API that will allow developers of in-line presentations to negotiate size and location and to redraw with the browser.

In this chapter, we examined XML tags and the logical and physical structure of an XML document which consists of elements and entities. Now that we have an understanding of how an XML document is structured, we turn our attention to how it is presented to the user for viewing.

Chapter 3

Doing It With Style

Now that we have some understanding of how an XML document is structured and organized, we can turn our attention to what we can do with it. The first and most important thing is to be able to read it and to display it for others to read. One of the strengths of HTML has been its ability to render documents in such a way that a variety of web browsers could interpret them for on-screen display or reformat them for printing, emailing, or exporting for use in other software applications.

Since the appearance of SGML, there have been various attempts to define a style language that would make it easy to interpret marked up text for rendering on paper or on screen. Because the eXtensible Style Language (XSL) builds on its predecessors used by SGML and HTML, we shall take a brief look at the Document Style Semantics and Specification Language (DSSSL) used by SGML and Cascading Style Sheets used in HTML before examining the eXtensible Style Language. We shall also examine some of the features of XML's style language. But, before we do so, we should consider the benefits to using style sheets which are the files that implement a style language and contain the layout settings for certain classes of documents.

Why Use Style Sheets

First of all, style sheets contain the layout settings for certain classes of documents in a separate file. A class of documents is a group of documents which share the same characteristics, such as memos, annual reports, budget proposals, monthly statements, etc. Storing style information in discrete files separates the layout settings from the document and its markup codes and dramatically simplifies the markup. A typical HTML page will have a lot of markup attributes which only specify how the content should appear on the screen. The tags must perform both content and display functions. This makes for cluttered pages, as display tags frequently taking up more physical space than the content itself. This also hinders achieving the real goal of the markup: to clarify the document's underlying structure.

Having the tags perform both content and display functions assumes that everything on the Web is designed for a single medium. This implies that only that medium will be able to "see" the whole Web as designed. If we change the characteristics of the display technology, a document could undergo a number of distortions. Take a document with columns or tables, for example. Converting it from one format to another or adjusting the margins, font, or type size can change the layout and appearance of the columns and tables, possibly rendering them incomprehensible.

A style sheet separates the content from its display characteristics, letting an author select a desired style specification for a given output medium without affecting the content or the markup. This also empowers the user to format a document based on his or her specific needs, such as for output to a braille printer or overhead projector instead of a computer screen. When a reader decides to print a page, he or she may want to re-style it to take advantage of the capabilities of the printed medium rather than print it as viewed on the monitor.

Style sheets also allow a number of documents to share a single style sheet. A style sheet is closely associated with a DTD, as the rules in a style sheet are targeted at specific elements. In fact, the DTD acts as a specification document for style sheet authors because it includes details about every element contained in the document and every possible contextual arrangement of these elements.

Coupling content and style makes it very difficult to customize a Web page for different "views" to accommodate different classes of users or a given user on different visits. Relatively advanced technology, such as cookies, Java applets and applications, server-side databases of user preferences, etc. can help do some of this; but these technologies all have drawbacks. Their main problem is that they are sufficiently advanced that only a relatively small number of practitioners and Web-site developers can use them effectively.

When the layout instructions are built into the document, we have an inflexible document which is designed for a particular display medium. It then becomes difficult to display the document any other way or to optimize the display to look good in every browser software or client application. By separating markup from content, an author can replace one style sheet with another one at any time, without editing the document itself. This would permit changing the style of a document in different ways, customized to various target audiences and media types, without editing the document itself.

Putting display-only tags into the markup has other drawbacks. It requires more work when an author wants to add elements with pre-defined attributes. These attributes must be entered manually or copied from previous instances. The author is also responsible for ensuring that the display-related attributes are used in a consistent manner to produce a document with a consistent look and feel. One could easily produce potential inconsistencies when making changes to certain elements or to the style of a page because it is harder to see the document's underlying structure when all the display information is included in the markup. It is also difficult to locate all the related elements when making changes.

While an author might be concerned primarily with delivering information over the Web in HTML, he or she might eventually find other uses for that information. Keeping the display-related information in a separate style sheet -- or even multiple style sheets -- permits re-using documents for a variety of purposes without having to modify the content. For example, one could produce a large-print version of a document for the visually impaired or create public and private versions of a document, restricting access to confidential details only to those who have the required access level. One could also create a preview version of a long document which would provide an abstract and a structured overview of the text.

The same document could be the source in all these cases. The style sheets associated with that document would control the differences without having to manually create different forms of each document. Style sheets give developers much flexibility in formatting and presenting their documents. They also provide limited ability to create their own formatting tag vocabularies.

The use of multiple style sheets allows authors to share some definitions. Authors can place common sets of rules in a separate style sheet to avoid unnecessary repetition. They can then refer to these style sheets at suitable locations in other style sheets. Now that we understand the importance of a style language and style sheets, we can turn our attention to some of the important milestones leading to the development of XSL.

Document Style Semantics and Specification Language (DSSSL)

The Formatting Output Specification Instance (FOSI, pronouced fosey) was the first style specification language. It was developed for use by the U.S. Department of Defense; but it did not meet with much success outside those circles because of its complexity. The Document Style Semantics and Specification Language (DSSSL) was developed almost at the same time as

FOSI. DSSSL is a very powerful and complex programming language for specifying the style of an SGML document.

DSSSL was probably too complicated for use on the Web; so a simplified version, known as DSSSL-Lite, was proposed. DSSSL-Lite was further modified for use on the Internet. This variation called DSSSL-o (short for DSSSL-online) was published in December, 1995, and reissued in August, 1996, with a few corrections. DSSSL-o, then, became the basis for the first version of XSL which we'll cover in more detail later.

DSSSL resembles SGML in its notation, using angle brackets and a hierarchical structure. For this reason, it is the preferred styling language for SGML documents and a natural candidate as the parent of choice for XSL, just as SGML is the parent of XML. But XSL and DSSSL are not an exact match as some XSL features have no counterpart in DSSSL.

Cascading Style Sheets

With the widespread use of HTML, the W3C prepared a recommendation for a style language designed specifically to define the presentation and appearance of an HTML document. Cascading Style Sheets (CSS), which became a W3C recommendation in December, 1996, allows authors to use style rules to define how HTML structural elements, such as paragraphs and headings, should be displayed without using additional HTML markup. CSS uses ASCII text, permitting authors to create and edit the style definitions easily in a standard text editor or word processor.

We shall not go into all the details of CSS. There are plenty of good books and Internet tutorials on how to use CSS style sheets. There are also many examples available on the Web to learn from. Rather, we are interested in the principles underlying CSS and how it influenced the development of XSL.

Some of CSS's features rely on encoding practices that are HTML-specific. For example, the anchor, <a>, linking element receives special treatment to distinguish visited links from unvisited ones. The "specification" may eventually become more generic and extended to apply to other DTDs. CSS cannot render tables very well as it has no settings for rows or columns; and it is almost impossible to create generic styles for building tables. CSS also lacks a wide variety of structural tools that more advanced style tools will include; but it is an important first step.

The W3C made a second level of Cascading Style Sheets official in May, 1998. This second level, CSS2, includes features to format tables, allowing users to style cells, rows, and columns in numerous ways. It is backwardly compatible with CSS1, meaning that all CSS1 style sheets will work under CSS2; and it follows the same general principles as CSS1:

Physical separation of the style information from the content that it describes; and

Syntactical separation of the style information from the document's markup codes used for other purposes.

Physical Separation

HTML lets an author place style information within a document; but browsers "read' and display HTML documents from top to bottom. This means that the style information needs to be at the top of the document to be effective. Placing a formatting instruction for a particular tag in the middle of a document, for example, will only affect the second half of the document. The first half will be governed by any pre-formatted codes or a default setting.

Keeping formatting instructions in a completely separate file from the document separates the different functions of the two kinds of information and makes it more convenient to maintain them. It also allows authors to use the same style information for other documents. This allows related documents, such as multiple pages across a site, to share the same look.

Syntactic separation

CSS formatting instructions don't resemble HTML or XML tags in any way. This makes it easy to distinguish style information from regular tags and attributes. However, it also means that one has to learn a completely new syntax to create formatting instructions.

Cascade

CSS1 and 2 follow a step-like arrangement (called a cascade, hence the designation in their title) in deciding which style rules to follow. The general principle is to use the most specific rules beginning with the style specified by an author, followed by any choices made by the user, and, finally, letting the browser apply its default styles if the other two don't specify anything. Thus, the stylistic decisions cascade or flow downhill from the author to the user to the browser.

While this process seems quite simple, it's usually more complicated. The CSS2 recommendation provides a sort of formula to resolve conflicts:

1. Read all available style specifications

This requires the browser to check each tag to determine if either the author or the user has specified a style for it. If not, it uses the default style for that tag. If only the author or only the user has specified a style, it uses that one. If both the author and the user specified a style, the browser "cascades" down to Rule #2

2. Look for "important" declarations

CSS1 and 2 allow authors and users to prevent their specifications from being overridden by a style specification for an element. The browser should follow either the author's or the user's style as designated. If neither has made such an indication, the browser "cascades" to rule #3.

3. Look for more specific declarations

When an author's and a user's style specifications conflict, the more specific declaration – the user's – wins. For example, if the author's style for a tag calls for displaying its content in a certain font family; and the user has specified that elements of that type should appear in a totally different font family, the browser will employ the specific font size and color designated by the user.

4. Rank by order received.

If conflicting style specifications from the same source – author, user, or agent – occur, they all have the same importance; and they share the same specificity. All other things being equal, the last specification is used. This rule acts as an absolute tie breaker because there can be only one "last" instruction. For example, if a style sheet has two conflicting formatting instructions for a heading tag, the browser will use the second one because it is the last instruction for that tag.

Accessing CSS Styles

Extensions to the HTML specification, to a large extent, have built-in mechanisms for attaching styles to an HTML document. And styles can cascade, allowing a user's linked style sheet to override a linked style sheet delivered with a document. CSS styles can be applied to HTML documents in three ways: the embedded method, the linked method, and the in-line method. The embedded style sheet approach places the style sheet at the top of the document, usually within the HTML Head element. The style specifications apply only to the document that contains them. The linked style sheet approach, on the other hand, stores the style sheet in a separate data file. Each document, then, simply refers to the remote style sheet through a Link element or by an "import" command.

Finally, the in-line style does not involve the concept of a style sheet at all. It is a rule that uses the HTML Style attribute applied directly to a specific instance of an element, such as:

```
<P style="color: blue">A blue paragraph</P>
```

CSS's 'cascading' feature can use these three approaches. For example, a style specified in an embedded style sheet can replace one defined in a linked style sheet. A style specified in an in-line style can, in turn, override the embedded style sheet. For example, a linked style sheet may specify that most Title elements in a set of documents should appear in bold typeface. However, an author can override this rule by using an embedded style sheet at the top of the document to indicate that titles in one document should appear in italic. One could also designate a title to appear in normal style by using a rule in the Title element concerned. This replaces all previous rules, but only for that particular title.

CSS Syntax

A style sheet consists of one or more rules which govern the handling and layout of elements. A collection of two or more rules is called a ruleset. Each rule contains two components: a selector and a property. The selector identifies the element whose content will be affected by the rule. A property is the visual or other characteristic that the selector will have after the rule has been applied. For example, if the selector's content is text, the rule can specify font family, size, and color as potential properties.

The general format of a rule is:

```
seletorlist { propertylist }
```

where the selectorlist consists of one or more tags without the surrounding angle brackets. The propertylist term, enclosed in "curly braces" rather than parentheses or square brackets, identifies one or more properties to apply to the tag(s) in the selectorlist. Multiple properties are separated with semicolons.

User Interface Controls

CSS2 contains some properties for customizing the user interface when browsing a document, or parts of one. One of these, the cursor property, allows changing the cursor to such things as crosshairs, a "pointing hand" that browsers use to indicate a hyperlink, an hourglass, clock face, or some other custom cursor shape. This just requires providing the URL of an image to be used, such as:

```
video { cursor: url("images/camera.cur") }
```

```
audio { cursor: url("images/speaker.cur") }
plotsummary { cursor: url("images/book.cur") }
```

The default cursor would then be replaced by a little movie camera icon when the mouse hovers over the <videoclip> element, a loudspeaker icon when over the <audioclip> element, and an "open book" image when over the contents of the <plotsummary> element. However, doing too much cursor-swapping, particularly with images that the browser normally cannot provide internally, can result in degradation of system performance. Users already have to wait to retrieve real content. Nobody wants to experience delays and messages like "Contacting site...Reading file..." just because they jostled the mouse a bit. However, as no two browsers interpret CSS in exactly the same way, developers look to the eXtensible Style Language as one way to achieve some degree of consistency.

eXtensible Style Language (XSL)

The XML recommendation describes the core language that specifies how to define XML documents and establishes the grammar that make documents comply with the XML specification. Two extensions have been proposed to extend XML beyond the core language: XML Linking Language (XLink), which we'll discuss in the next chapter, and eXtensible Stylesheet Language (XSL). Microsoft, AborText, and Inso Corporation proposed XSL to the W3C in the fall of 1997 in hopes of making it the standard style language for XML documents. XSL is based on DSSSL which is more of a processing language than a style language; but it will use XML syntax rather than DSSSL. In fact, DSSSL is a superset to XSL, just as SGML is a superset of XML.

DSSSL attempted to define rules for displaying SGML-tagged data and to provide a superset of the Cascading Style Sheets functionality. XSL retained a lot of the original DSSSL concepts and completely changed DSSSL's syntax which was derived from LISP. XSL uses the same syntax as XML, making XML's style language as accessible to computer processing and generation as the XML language itself. XSL will be able to generate CSS along with HTML and handle the translation of XML-based data to HTML or other presentation formats.

XSL is still in the working draft stage. The most recent version at the time of this writing is dated April 21, 1999. Even when completed, it will be quite a while before it receives widespread support. In the meantime, CSS remains the lowest common denominator of all style languages and has the best support. In the short term, rendering XML using CSS can be a viable alternative to waiting, even though DSSSL can also be applied to XML documents.

CSS can be implemented easily with XML with only minor modifications to a DTD. For example, a developer can add a CDATA STYLE attribute to individual elements to add style information. CSS also formulates its rules in terms of element names, IDs, and so on, which XML and HTML documents also use. The W3C published its recommendation Associating Style Sheets with XML on June 29, 1999. This recommendation specifies how to use style sheets like CSS or DSSSL with XML. Developers can thus use CSS to begin creating style sheets for XML documents and store formatting information separately from their content until the completion of the XSL recommendation.

Declaring a CSS for XML Documents

To tell a browser how to display an XML document using a CSS requires informing the browser where to find the style sheet. This is done by including, at the top of the XML document, a processing instruction with a URL which points to the style sheet, something like this:

<?XML-stylesheet type="text/css" href=sheet-name.css"?>

The value in the "type" specification indicates that the document being pointed to contains text and that the text contains CSS formatting instructions. This declaration is a MIME-type declaration. (MIME is an acronym for the Multi-purpose Internet Mail Extensions standard for Internet content formats.) The "href" statement identifies the URL of the style sheet itself.

An XML-aware browser will recognize a suitable CSS style sheet to display an XML document. However, an HTML-aware browser will require a software 'filter' to transform an SGML or XML document into HTML format to display.

XSL, when completed, will provide the display semantics for XML by mapping XML into HTML or any other formatting language. Display issues such as font, justification, color, etc. will be handled by style sheets. XSL will also allow developers to build a presentation structure that differs from the original data structure because the data and its presentation style will be two separate entities. This will allow authors to format and display data elements in multiple places on a page, rearrange them, or remove them. For example, the same bibliographic data source could be used to create a catalog, a bibliography, a footnote, a citation, a purchase order, or an invoice merely by changing the style sheet, without modifying the data.

XSL'sParts

XSL consists of two parts:

1. a language for transforming XML documents, and

2. an XML vocabulary for specifying formatting semantics.

The first part, XSL Transformations (XSLT) Specification Version 1.0. deals with the syntax and semantics for XSL and how to apply style sheets to transform one document into another. The second part (Extensible Stylesheet Language (XSL) Specification) is concerned with the XSL formatting objects, their attributes, and how they can be combined. XSL's formatting objects are based on those used by CSS and DSSSL; but XSL is designed to be easier to use than DSSSL.

One of the unique features of XSL is that while CSS can be used to style HTML documents, XSL can transform XML documents into other XML documents. For example, XSL can be used to transform XML data into HTML/CSS documents on the Web server. This way, the two languages complement each other and can be used together. Both languages can be used to style XML documents. CSS and XSL will use the same underlying formatting model and designers will therefore have access to the same formatting features in both languages.

Those who are familiar with regular XML documents will be able to understand XSL's syntax easily. XSL extends much of XML's markup syntax to styles and uses the familiar angle bracket (< and >) characters and attribute-value specifications. CSS, on the other hand, uses a different syntax with curly braces, colons, semi-colons, and commas, as well as different rules for their use.

CSS2 is generally not aware of a document's structure, even if it contains a few features which acknowledge that elements contain other elements and don't exist in a vacuum. In CSS2, styles apply to elements, not to portions of the element tree which is why it works equally well with XML and HTML. XSL, on the other hand, reverses this priority. XSL style sheets look like the XML documents they refer to and permit re-designing the appearance of a document in such a way that its resulting structure can appear totally different from the original document.

CSS will likely co-exist with XSL because they meet different needs. CSS is intended for dynamic formatting of online documents for multiple media. Its strictly declarative nature limits its capabilities but also makes it efficient and easy to generate and modify in the content-generation workflow. XSL, on the other hand, is intended for complex formatting where the content of the document might be displayed in multiple places. For example, the text of a heading might also appear in a dynamically generated table of contents. So they are two different tools. CSS is the appropriate choice for some tasks and XSL for others. They can also be used together, such as XSL on a server to condense or customize some XML data into a simpler XML document which is then formatted on the client with CSS.

Flow Objects

One of the important concepts -- probably the single most important concept to understand to use XSL -- that XSL retains from DSSSL -- is that of "flow objects." A flow object is a portion of a document, sometimes called a "chunk," which is displayed as a single unit. For example, we generally want to manipulate a paragraph or an image as a single unit, formatting the entire paragraph in a particular font or placing an image on the screen at a particular point. The complete set of flow objects that make up an XML document is known as a "flow object tree." Each flow object has characteristics such as font-name and font-size that can be specified explicitly or inherited from flow objects further up the flow object tree.

The style engine passes the flow object tree to the XML processor. This flow object tree, created by merging the source document with the style sheet instructions, contains the flow objects. These flow objects represent display elements (paragraphs, tables, table rows, characters, and so on) and the relationships of one flow object to another. Just as with a family tree, the document is a flow object tree. The document as a whole is the root. Its elements and subelements branch off from that root as child elements. The child elements may themselves be parents to other child elements, which may contain children of their own, and so forth. XSL considers the positions of flow objects (elements) within the entire document to produce very flexible rules for applying formatting.

Thus, a simple HTML document might look like this:

```
<HTML>
        <HEAD>
                <TITLE>[Text to be used as title]</TITLE>
        </HEAD>
        <BODY><P>This is a paragraph...</P>
                <TABLE>[Various table elements]</TABLE>
        </BODY>
</HTML>
```

Most of the elements in this example are separate flow objects. The <HEAD> and <BODY> elements are not flow objects, however, because they don't have display characteristics. The elements they contain, however, are flow objects. One can then display these flow objects in many different ways.

Flow objects can also be grouped into hierarchies of flow objects. For example, a chapter contains many paragraphs. Nesting things within other things resembles the structure of an XML document except that a flow object represents how a logical (structural) document component is to be displayed.

XML itself does not have any flow objects; so XSL needs a standard set of them into which to "pour" an XML document's flow object tree. Instead of starting from scratch to define whole new flow objects, the authors of XSL adapted two existing sets: those available in HTML/CSS and those available in DSSSL. But they did not use all of these flow objects in XSL. The ones they did incorporate are referred to as "core flow objects" of the source language (e.g. HTML core flow object).

XSL also has its own list of flow objects, called formatting objects which are designated fo:[name]. It is important to note that formatting objects are the least supported feature of XSL and have undergone the most change in recent drafts.

The definition of each formatting object is intended to provide the following information: (1) an overview of the role of the formatting object, (2) the semantics of the formatting object, and (3) a listing of the properties and content applicable to the formatting object. The formatting semantics of the formatting object are specified by "reducing" the properties and content of the formatting object to one or more areas within the formatting model. There are several aspects to this reduction. The content of the formatting object is "distributed" into the areas "generated" in the reduction. The semantics do not specify any particular method for achieving the distribution of the content into areas, but instead specify a set of "constraints" which the distribution must satisfy.

The constraints are most often expressed in terms of properties on the formatting object for which the content is being distributed; for example, that the content of a flow object must be kept with the content of the previous or next flow object. Some constraints, however, are derived from the structure of the result tree or the formatting object itself; for example, which type of areas are generated to hold the content. The definition of each formatting object specifies what constraints must be satisfied.

XSL Style Sheet Processor

XSL provides a capability similar to "mail merge." The style sheet contains a template specifying how the document should look; and it identifies data in the source document to insert into this template. This model for merging data and templates is referred to as the template-driven model and works well on regular and repetitive data.

An XSL style sheet processor reads the XML document or data and formats the content as directed by the style sheet. This process involves two steps. First, the processor constructs a result tree from the XML source tree, a process called tree transformation. Second, the processor interprets the result tree to produce a formatted presentation to display on a computer monitor, print on paper, output to a speech synthesizer or some other media. This second process is called formatting and is performed by the formatter.

Breaking the processing of a style sheet into two steps permits greater flexibility in constructing the presentation of the source content. The tree transformation step allows the structure of the result tree to be totally different from the structure of the source tree. This allows filtering and reordering the result tree in ways that are radically different from the source tree. One can also modify the structure and add generated content, such as a table-of-contents. One could also map the result of a database query (expressed in XML) into a sorted tabular presentation. The tree transformation process constructs the result tree and adds the information (formatting semantics) necessary to format that result tree.

The formatting process reads the formatting semantics which appear as a catalog of formatting objects. Each node of the result tree is a formatting object which denotes how the page, paragraph, footnote, etc. will appear. An author can use a set of formatting properties, such as indents; word- and letter-spacing; and widow, orphan, and hyphenation control to get finer control over the presentation. Together, the formatting objects and formatting properties provide the vocabulary for expressing presentation intent.

XSL also provides capabilities for handling highly irregular and recursive data such as is typical in documents. Template fragments are defined; and the XSL processor combines the results of these fragments into a final result tree based on the shape of the source data. Each template fragment declares the type and context of source nodes it is appropriate for, allowing the XSL processor to match source nodes with template fragments.

Microsoft's XML processor, which is part of Internet Explorer 5, supports XSL. It transforms XML into HTML, which is then displayed using CSS; but it does not implement formatting objects. (See http://msdn.microsoft.com/xml/XSLGuide/xsl-overview.asp for more information.)

Anatomy of an XSL Style Sheet

An XSL style sheet, also called a transform, uses the XML namespaces mechanism to recognize XSLT-defined elements. These elements all begin with a prefix of xsl: to identify them to the XSLT processor for use only in the style sheet, not in the source document. The names of XSLT elements, attributes, and functions are all lower-case, with hyphens separating words.

This example shows the structure of a style sheet. (Compare it with the example in Appendix 4.) Ellipses (...) indicate where attribute values or content have been omitted. Although this example shows one of each type of allowed element, style sheets may contain zero or more of each of these elements.

```
<xsl:stylesheet xmlns:xsl="http://www.w3.org/XSL/Transform/1.0">

 <xsl:import href="..."/>

 <xsl:include href="..."/>

 <xsl:strip-space elements="..."/>

 <xsl:preserve-space elements="..."/>

 <xsl:output method="..."/>

 <xsl:key name="..." match="..." use="..."/>

 <xsl:locale name="...">
 ...
 </xsl:locale>

 <xsl:attribute-set name="...">
 ...
 </xsl:attribute-set>

 <xsl:variable name="...">...</xsl:variable>

 <xsl:param name="...">...</xsl:param>

 <xsl:template match="...">
 ...
 </xsl:template>

 <xsl:template name="...">
 ...
 </xsl:template>

</xsl:stylesheet>
```

Construction Rules

An XSL style sheet, like a CSS2 style sheet, typically consists of two types of rules: construction rules and style rules. A tree construction rule maps an element type to a flow object type. The element's characteristics are represented by attributes; and the names of the elements and attributes reflect the flow object and characteristic names defined in the DSSSL standard.

A construction rule has two parts: a pattern that is matched against elements in the source tree and a template that constructs a portion of the result tree. Each object in the document tree can match only one construction rule; but a single construction rule may create several flow objects. Construction rules allow a style sheet to be applicable to a wide class of documents that have similar source tree structures. A construction rule creates an element or pattern, such as a division using the <DIV>... </DIV> tags. The pattern resembles a series of XSL elements, each with an attribute that names the element in the XML document to which the action will be applied. The Tree Construction is described in "XSL Transformations (XSLT)" (http://www.w3.org/1999/08/WD-xslt-19990813).

An example of an XSL construction rule with target elements for a book might look something like this:

```
<xsl>
        <rule>
        <target-element type="book"/>
        <DIV> font-size="14pt"; font-family="serif">
        <children/>
        </DIV>
        </rule>
</xsl>
```

The rule constructs a pattern of a book element, <target-element type="book"/>. Each element of the type "book" will receive the font characteristics (font size of 14 points and the serif font family) specified within the division specified with the <DIV>... </DIV> tags. The <DIV> tag indicates divisions in a document and can be used to group block elements together. Because the <DIV>... </DIV> tags include the <children/> tag, the rule also applies to all the child elements of the type "book."

The second part of the construction rule is the action. It specifies actions to perform when an element which matches the condition laid out in the pattern is encountered. In other words, one can tell XML that every time it finds a particular pattern, it should take a specified action. The actions in construction rules don't actually apply a style to an element. Instead, they create flow objects. The target element is transformed into the flow object which has the desired style.

The first rule in an XSL style sheet usually defines a style for the top-level flow object produced from the target XML document. Even if this flow object has no special styling, it is a good idea to include this so-called root rule, as it tells the XSL application where to begin. A typical XSL document looks schematically like this:

```
<fo:root>
      <rule>
            {construction rule1]
            {construction rule2]
. . .
      </rule>
      <rule>
            {construction rule3]
. . .
      </rule>
. . .
</fo:root>
```

The pair of <fo:root> and </fo:root> tags define the root element of the XSL document. (The fo: prefix denotes a formatting object.) The rule specifies the pattern or element to look for and one or more actions to perform when the pattern is encountered. Each action in a construction rule is a flow object coupled with particular display characteristics. These display characteristics appear as attribute-value pairs for the flow object element. If an element in the target document doesn't have any styling specified for it, XSL comes with a built-in default rule.

Construction rules have much more power when used with XSL than with CSS2. XSL understands and works better with element trees than CSS2. It also has advanced features that offer the ability to do things like reordering branches of the tree into a flow-object tree that is entirely different in structure from the XML document itself. It allows grabbing a related piece of text from elsewhere in the document, for example, so an author can create a table of contents from the chapter headings and place it at the beginning of the displayed document. One can also easily suppress parts of a document that should not display at a certain time. The core expression language also includes mathematical functions that make it easy to express font sizes, spacing, and so on, in relative rather than absolute terms. This means that one can write style sheets that allow the user to blow up the whole display in a consistent manner by overriding the base font size.

Style Rules

A style rule, also called a template, contains a pattern and an action expressed in XML form, such as:

```
<style-rule>
      [pattern]
      [action]
</style-rule>
```

It specifies the action to take when the pattern is encountered. The pattern can consist of a simple target-element or a target-element nested in another element. The style rule's pattern can select elements on the basis of their attributes, just as a construction rule; but the style rule's action is much simpler than its counterpart can be in a construction rule. In fact, it can only have one possible action with many possible variations. An element in the action portion of a style rule has as many attributes as there are "things" that the author wants to format.

For example, an XSL rule defines the presentation and appearance of an XML document's target elements:

```
<xsl>
      <style-rule>
      <target-element type="title"/>
      <apply font-weight="italic"/>
      </style-rule>
</xsl>
```

The style rule begins and ends with the pair of <xsl>...</xsl> tags, just as style definitions for an HTML document are encloses within a pair of <STYLE>...</STYLE> tags in CSS. This XSL style rule indicates that the pattern or target element (the element to which the style rule will apply) is a title. Whenever the processor encounters a title, then, it applies an italic font to it.

XSL creates formatting structures for both elements and documents. It lets developers create styles that understand an element's uniqueness and provides the ability to modify it based on its position in a document, its ancestry (by which other elements it is contained), or its relation to other elements. Developers will usually only need the declarative XSL markup; but they can also supplement their styles with EcmaScript (formerly JavaScript) code. They can also extend XSL style sheets into formatting macros.

Processing

It is rarely sufficient to simply map a style rule to all elements with a particular name. An author may want to change the format depending on where the element occurs in the document. Sometimes, an element's format depends on which other element contains it. An author can match elements by ID, element name, ancestry, children, and attributes to apply a style to a particular element instance or to a context defining element. For example, one may want to apply a particular style to an element when it is the only child of another element or when it is the first or last element in a sequence. One can also consider only elements with the same name when applying one of these constraints. By using an element's position attribute to qualify the patterns within the style rules, one can specify the element's position with respect to its siblings. The valid values for position are:

first-of-type: the element must be the first sibling of its type
last-of-type: the element must be the last sibling of its type
first-of- any: the element must be the first sibling element
last-of- any: the element must be the last sibling element
only-of-any: the element must not have any sibling elements
only-of-type: the element must not have any sibling elements of the same type
not-first-of-any: the element must not be the first sibling element
not-last-of- any: the element must not be the last sibling element
not-last-of-type: the element must not be the last sibling of its type
not-only-of-any: the element must have one or more sibling elements
not-only-of-type: the element must have one or more sibling elements of the same type

The following example shows how the position attribute might be used to make the first occurrence of the element of type book appear in italics. Subsequent occurrences would remain in the default font.

```
<xsl>
      <style-rule>
      <target-element type="book" position="first-of-type"/>
      <apply font-weight="italic"/>
      </style-rule>
</xsl>
```

Authors have three options for processing style rules: direct processing, restricted processing,, and conditional processing. Direct processing is appropriate if the XML document has a known, regular structure such as tables and catalogs. An author can process each item recursively down the tree by using the for-each statement. Alternatively, one could restrict processing to certain children of an element by using the xsl:apply-templates instruction, <xsl:apply-templates/>, and then selecting the elements to be processed by their names. XSL has two instructions for conditional processing: xsl:if and xsl:choose. The xsl:if instruction works much the same way as the if...then statements in BASIC and most other programs by providing simple if (a), then (b) conditionality. The xsl:choose instruction enables selecting one choice from several possibilities. It consists of a series of xsl:when elements followed by an optional xsl:otherwise element. When the processor encounters an xsl:choose element, it tests each of the xsl:when elements in turn. When it hits the first, and only the first xsl:when element which tests true, it selects and uses that element. If it does not encounter any xsl:when element that satisfies the condition and if there is no xsl:otherwise element present, nothing is created.

Sorting

One can sort elements by adding xsl:sort elements as children of xsl:apply-templates or xsl:for-each elements (see Appendix 4). (The xsl:for-each element sets up a loop and repeats a block of code as long as a particular condition is true.) The first xsl:sort child specifies the primary sort key, the second xsl:sort child specifies the secondary sort key, and so on. When an xsl:apply-templates or a xsl:for-each instruction contains one or more xsl:sort children, then the XML processor sorts those elements according to the specified sort keys and processes them in the sorted order instead of processing the selected elements in the order they appear in the XML document. xsl:sort elements must occur first when used in an xsl:for-each element,.

An xsl:sort statement has a select attribute with a value that is a select pattern. For each element to be processed, the select pattern is evaluated with that element as the current element. The value of the first selected element is used as the sort key for that element. The default value of the select attribute is '.' which will cause the string-value of the current node to be used as the sort key. This string serves as a sort key. The following optional attributes of xsl:sort control how the list of sort keys are sorted:

> order – Specifies whether the strings should be sorted in ascending or descending order; ascending specifies ascending order; descending specifies descending order; the default is ascending.
>
> lang – Specifies the language of the sort keys; it has the same range of values as the xml:lang attribute; if no lang value is specified, the language is determined from the system environment.
>
> data-type – Specifies the data type of the sort strings; the following values are allowed:
>
>> text – Specifies that the sort keys should be sorted alphabetically in the correct manner for the language specified by lang.
>>
>> number – Specifies that the sort keys are to be converted into numbers and then sorted according to their numeric values; the value specified by lang can be used to help convert the values into numbers. The default value is text.

case-order – This can have the value upper-first or lower-first. This value applies when data-type="text" and specifies that the uppercase characters should be sorted before the lowercase letters, or vice versa respectively. For example, if lang="en", then A a B b are sorted with case-order="upper-first" and a A b B are sorted with case-order="lower-first". The default value is language dependent.

Naming Styles

Sometimes construction and style rules use a group of specific characteristic values frequently. While it is possible to embed a style rule within an attribute, this approach requires repeating the rule each time the element is used. This wastes disk space, memory, network bandwidth, and human effort.

XSL allows "wrapping" these style values into a style object and naming them, much like a macro. The Define Style element contains attributes for each common characteristic, plus a Name attribute to name the style group. The use of a named style in a rule's action varies, depending on the type of rule. A construction rule employs the style group through the Use attribute. A style rule, on the other hand, refers to the style group by using the Apply element. The Apply element contains an element whose name matches the value of the name attribute of the named style. When the processor encounters the Apply element, it replaces it with the attribute specified in the named style.

XSL permits defining named styles and inline styles as well as scripts and macros for use in XSL style sheets. Inline styles are useful to style only one or two of the elements in the XML document without having to create a complete XSL file. An inline style can also serve to declare a style for an element in the XML document itself. It is also possible to include one style sheet inside another by using a processing instruction to name and locate the style sheet to include at that location. The processor then uses the rules in the remote style sheet as if they were in the main style sheet. The <import/> tag, e.g. <import href="mystyle.xsl">, imports one XSL style sheet into another XSL style sheet to nest them one inside the other.

Scripts and Macros

XSL has made a big improvement over what's possible with CSS2 by including scripting capabilities. Scripting allows including programs and function calls that affect the style in various ways. The <define-script> ... </define-script> tag permits writing scripts that define both functions and variables. XSL supports ECMAScript (formerly known as JavaScript), the programming language that is the Web standard for lighter-weight applications. The scripts can then be used in a construction or style rule.

One can also define a macro with the <define-macro> ... </define-macro> tag. A macro can break a style sheet into named parts, group HTML and CSS objects together, or define common groups of flow objects -- or more complex single flow objects for reuse across multiple rules in the style sheet. It can also serve to remove any duplication and clarify the style sheet design when a group of characteristics have the same or similar values in several different rules. Once defined, the macro can be used in the action portion of a construction rule simply by using the macro's name as an element name, along with any additional style attributes.

Creating Style Sheets

ArborText's XML Styler is one example of a graphical user interface (GUI) tool to create, edit, and manipulate XML style sheets. It makes it easy to create XSL style sheets because it eliminates the need to remember the syntax of the different XSL commands for creating patterns, actions, and so on. Written in standard Java, XML Styler is available for download from the ArborText Web site at www.arbortext.com. The product is "bound" into a WIN32 executable that uses the Microsoft Java Virtual Machine (JVM). It runs on the Windows 95 and Windows NT platforms only and requires Internet Explorer 4.x. ArborText plans to release an "unbound" version of XML Styler, which will run with the Sun JVM (or others).

Transformis produces Stylus, an integrated development environment for XSL stylesheets; and an XSL processor is available for free download from http://www.inria.fr/koala/XML/xslProcessor. This tool is a Java XSL processor that takes an XSL file and an XML file and creates one or more HTML files. Eventually, most word processors will support XML as a native format; so converting and styling XML documents will become a standard operating procedure.

Work-Arounds

Some companies eager to implement XML have had to resort to temporary work-arounds to display XML documents until XSL becomes finalized. One such company is CatchWord (http://www.catchword.com). CatchWord, founded in 1994, provides libraries with a database of online journals from thirty-six scholarly, academic, and business publishers. It provides libraries with IP address validation, multi-format delivery options, advanced search facilities, document to document reference linking, and document delivery service.

CatchWord has made the content of all its service available in XML format since April, 1999. The company receives the journal in Postscript or Adobe Acrobat (PDF) format. It then analyzes those files to identify characters, positions, fonts, and structure before converting them for delivery via the Internet. Readers can receive the articles in PDF, RealPage, or VML format. (Microsoft's page description language which resembles XML and serves as an XSL stand-in until it becomes finalized.) Subscribers will soon be able to receive the articles in PGML format also. CatchWord does not code the full text in SGML or XML but renders its internal page description to XML aware browsers. Readers, then use Adobe Acrobat, the RealPage Viewer, or Internet Explorer 5 to view the articles.

References in articles have usually been a major source of information for scholars and researchers seeking to pursue a topic. In the print world, this effort generally requires further searches of pertinent bibliographic resources such as library catalogs, abstracting and indexing services, or even interlibrary loan or document delivery if the library does not have the desired reference. CatchWord's Active Reference Linking technology incorporates the appropriate links, allowing researchers to navigate seamlessly from article to article irrespective of the journal title or publisher. Researchers can do full text searching across an article, a journal, or a discipline. When linking directly to the full text is not possible because the company does not hold a particular title, there are links to the most appropriate external resources, typically an abstracting and indexing service that can provide further information, such as an abstract.

The Active Reference Links are built into the documents in the collection irrespective of the format in which they are delivered to the end user – PDF, RealPage, or XML. They are also automatically updated as new abstracting and indexing services are added. This prevents "link rot" where the links go out of date or fail to point to relevant citations. CatchWord is building interfaces with the major abstracting and indexing services and subscription agents. These include OCLC, Cambridge Scientific Abstracts, SilverPlatter, Anbar Abstracts, and ISI's Web of Science. The company will also work with libraries to provide access from Web-based on-line public access catalogs (OPACs) or other Web-based resources.

Multimedia Style Sheets

Aural style sheets

Tools like XML Styler or conversion utilities in word processors concentrate on the production of textual documents in XML format. However, not all communication media are textual in nature; and there is a need for access to information by vision-impaired people. The W3C community has been concerned about access to information, particularly via the Web, by means other than the standard video display computer monitor. CSS2 permits the use of special properties that "render" elements audibly rather than visually. While such aural style sheets are targeted primarily for use by the blind or visually impaired, they can also be used for special-purpose applications such as conference presentations, in-car Web browsing systems, or other applications where the user must focus visually on something else, such as a surgeon needing a specific piece of information during an operation.

Suppose we want to create a document with clips of an interview with an author. An element, such as <dialog> could contain the audio portions capable of being read aloud. A basic, non-aural rule for the element might look something like this in CSS2:

```
dialog { font-size: medium }
```

But this rule has no meaning in an aural context; so we could specify other properties that do make sense, such as:

```
dialog { speak: normal; volume: normal; voice-family: cronkite; cue-
before: url ("intro.au") }
```

This instruction tells the speech-to-text converter to read the content of the <dialog> element aloud, in a normal volume. It also specifies to use the cronkite voice family (which is characterized by the CSS2 spec as "a kind of 'audio font'"). It further indicates that an audio cue should be played before beginning the dialog. This cue could consist of a simple bell, "ding," or other audio indication that a reading is about to begin such as a recording which says something like, "dialog beginning!"

There are several programs that "read" text from a computer monitor. There's even a category of voice browser technologies emerging. Motorola's offering, called VoxML for Voice Markup Language, provides users with voice-based access to Web content via either a voice browser or a standard telephone. The voice browser interprets voice the way Web browsers interpret HTML. Users can access Web content via voice prompts and receive the content in audio form via text-to-speech conversion or prerecorded clips. Not to be outdone, IBM developed SpeechML (Speech Markup Language) which is similar to VoxML. As with VoxML, SpeechML also aims to provide access to Web content via the telephone.

Microsoft, Compaq, and Macromedia, Inc. submitted another application, HTML+TIME, to the W3C for consideration. TIME stands for Timed Interactive Multimedia Extensions. Like the Synchronized Multimedia Integration Language (SMIL), described below, TIME makes it easy to include multimedia events in Web pages. It defines a set of multimedia extensions that add timing, interaction, and streaming media capabilities to HTML. It allows integrating time-based media, such as audio, video, and animation directly into Web pages, without relying on external multimedia players.

Text-to-speech converters have a notorious problem with words that aren't pronounced the way the software might expect. Acronyms; proper nouns, such as people's names; jargon; and words in a language other than what the software is tuned to "hear" are obvious examples. An aural style sheet could instruct the software to spell out an element's contents if the software may not interpret it properly.

SMIL

Multimedia elements are becoming increasingly more important for communication. To this end, the W3C has approved a recommendation that allows integrating a set of independent multimedia objects into a synchronized multimedia presentation. This recommendation, called the Synchronized Multimedia Integration Language (SMIL 1.0, pronounced "smile") lets an author

1. describe the temporal behavior of the presentation
2. describe the layout of the presentation on a screen
3. associate hyperlinks with media objects

SMIL documents are XML 1.0 documents and require some familiarity with the concepts and terms defined in XML 1.0. The "layout" element determines how the elements in the document's body are positioned on an abstract rendering surface (either visual or acoustic). If a document contains no layout element, the positioning of the body elements will depend on the implementation program.

A SMIL document can contain multiple alternative layouts by enclosing several layout elements within a "switch" element which can be used, for example, to describe the document's layout using different layout languages. SMIL's basic layout is consistent with the visual rendering model defined in CSS2. It reuses the formatting properties defined by the CSS2 specification and newly introduces the "fit" attribute [CSS2].

SMIL defines a link element, similar to the <LINK> tag in HTML. This link element lets an author describe navigational links between objects. All links in SMIL are actuated by the user. SMIL is based on the linking concepts of the XML Linking Language (XLL) which we'll discuss in the next chapter. It takes some the basic concepts of XLL and puts restrictions on them, such as restrictions to in-line links and limitations to uni-directional, single-headed links. In other words, all links have one source and one destination resource, such as the links in HTML with the <a> element type.

We began this chapter by explaining the importance and rationale of a style language that separates the markup from the style rules. We then took a brief look at the Document Style Semantics and Specification Language used by

SGML and Cascading Style Sheets used in HTML which have contributed to the development of the eXtensible Style Language. We then examined some of the features of XML's style language. We considered the concept of flow objects and the construction and style rules that make up an XSL style sheet. We looked at some tools to create XSL style sheets and what one company, CatchWord, is doing in the meantime until the language becomes formalized. We also considered, briefly, some of the efforts of the W3C to accommodate multimedia elements for dissemination via the Internet. Now, we turn our attention to the third portion of the eXtensible Markup Language: its capabilities for pointing and linking.

Chapter 4

Pointing and Linking

SGML does not support hyperlinking, usually referred to as linking, in its markup language. Linking is specific to HTML. It is the feature that makes HTML so valuable for navigating the Internet and makes the Internet such a rich resource. To be viable as an Internet technology, XML needs its own linking mechanism which will be backwardly compatible with existing HTML linking mechanisms. It also has to support the extensibility and robustness inherent to XML.

XML supports links similar to those in HTML; but it is more powerful in that the links can be both unidirectional and multidirectional. While HTML links access documents at the page level (an entire page at a time), XML links can address a document at the object level, such as a single paragraph or section, thus enhancing the hypertext links that make the Web work.

XML's Linking Language (XLL) is the third major piece of the XML specification. It was first proposed in August, 1997; but the W3C renamed it to XLink in March, 1998 and split the original proposal into three separate documents: a statement of design principles, the XML Linking Language specification (now called XLink), and the XML Pointer Language (XPointer). These three documents, which are still in working draft status at the time of this writing, now make up XML's Linking Language.

In this chapter, we shall begin with an overview of XLink, XPointer, and XPath. We shall then briefly discuss HTML links which can help us to understand XML links. We shall proceed to XML links and discuss how they compare with HTML links. We shall examine the differences between simple and extended links and how links are built. This will involve a treatment of the various attributes and their meanings. We shall also talk about remapping attributes to avoid conflicts and the use of extended link groups. While XLink deals with links to resources, XPointer deals with resources that are contained within XML documents. In this section, we shall examine how to identify and link to document fragments. We shall discuss three ways to address a link (absolute keywords, relative keywords, and string matching) and the use of interactive pointers. Finally, we shall briefly examine XPath which is the language for addressing parts of an XML document. We shall consider the different node types that XPath recognizes, absolute and relative location paths, and navigation. As the drafts of the three XLL documents use lowercase letters for their attributes and keywords, we shall implement that practice in this chapter.

Overview

XML Linking Language (XLL) is the broad term for XML hyperlinking that includes both linking and addressing. Renamed XLink, it "specifies constructs that may be inserted into XML resources to describe links between objects. A link, as the term is used here, is an explicit relationship between two or more data objects or portions of data objects." XLink uses XML syntax to create structures that can describe the simple unidirectional hyperlinks of today's HTML as well as more sophisticated multi-ended and typed links. (Typed links are those that fall into type categories, such as http links or binary relationships.)

XPointer is the companion specification that defines a language which is expected to be used with XLink. It "builds upon the XML Path Language (XPath) to support addressing into the internal structures of XML documents." It also defines the constructs that support such addressing. In particular, it provides for specific reference to elements, character strings, and other parts of XML documents, whether or not they bear an explicit ID attribute; using traversals of a document's structure; and choice of parts based on their properties such as element types, attribute values, character content, and relative position, containment, and order. XLink directs how to insert links into an XML document to point to something like another document or an image. XPointer, on the other hand, defines the fragment identifier that goes on a URL when linking to an XML document.

XPath is a language for addressing parts of an XML document. Designed to be used by both XSLT (XSL Transformations) and XPointer, XPath is the result of an effort to provide a common syntax and semantics for functionality shared between XSL Transformations and XPointer. Its primary purpose is to address parts of an XML document by providing basic facilities for manipulation of strings, numbers and booleans (true/false expressions). XPath uses a compact, non-XML syntax to facilitate the use of XPath within URIs and XML attribute values. XPath operates on the abstract, logical structure of an XML document, rather than on its surface syntax, modeling an XML document as a tree of nodes.

XPath gets its name from its use of a path notation as in URLs for navigating through the hierarchical structure of an XML document.

HTML Links

Before we can understand how links work in XLink, we need to know how they work in HTML. HTML permits one document to point to another by using only two element types: the anchor tag, "<A>," which surrounds the text or image that one wants to link from and the corresponding <LINK> tag. Then, one can link to another location in the current page, another document or to another site on the Web by using the LINK HREF="URL" attribute to specify a document or a specific point in the document that one wants to link to, as in the following example that links to the eXtensible Style Language (XSL) document:

<A HREF="http://www.w3.org/TR/NOTE-XSL-970910/A>

The anchor tag has several attributes; but only one gets constant use -- the all-powerful HREF which always takes a URL as its value and which represents the target of the link. A URL may be either absolute or relative. An absolute URL begins by identifying the protocol that should be used to interpret the URL. Common protocols include:

http: (Hypertext Transfer Protocol)
ftp: (File Transfer Protocol)
gopher: (the Gopher protocol)
mailto: (Electronic mail address)
file: (Host-specific file names)
telnet: (Reference to interactive sessions)
wais: (Wide Area Information Servers)
news: (USENET news)
nntp: (USENET news containing NNTP access)
prospero: (Prospero Directory Service)

Then comes the information applicable to the protocol. This usually consists of a reference to a server or a file on a server, prefixed with two slashes (//). The header information also contains the link elements which indicate the relationships between the HTML document as a whole and other resources. One could also include a question mark in a URL for searching.

In addition to using absolute addresses to locate a document, HTML also supports relative addresses which omit the full path to the file or resource and just give the file name. This lets the browser search for the resource. A relative URL is more flexible than an absolute URL because it allows moving resources without editing the entity declarations. However, it takes longer to execute and may not find its target.

XML Links

Terminology

Before we begin to discuss linking in XML, we need to explain some of the terminology, as it differs from that used in SGML and HTML.

HTML refers to links as sources and targets because the links go only in one direction, much like a one-way street. XLink is much more powerful than HTML's hyperlinks because the links can be bidirectional. This means that the end of a link could be both a source and a target. Consequently, XLink refers to linking elements instead of sources and to resources instead of targets.

A resource is anything that could be involved in a link: an XML document, parts of (and points within) documents, images, programs, a piece of data, the result of a database query, or an external link that acts as an intermediary to a final destination. As with HTML, a resource could include other parts of the same document, HTML documents, images, and other multimedia files, and so on.

The document at the "from" end of the link is called the local resource, while the destination of the link, the document on the "to" end, is called the remote resource. These terms do not necessarily imply that the resources reside on a local or remote computer or server. "Local" just means "here;" and remote just means "there" – even if "there" is on the same physical computer or within the same document as the local resource.

A resource might have a caption associated with it to explain to a human reader the significance of the resource in the link. This caption is call a title.

The special element within an XML document that declares the existence of a link and contains a description of the link's characteristics is called a linking element.

The part of the link that identifies where to find the resource is called a locator. The locator is a character string that appears in a linking element. It usually consists of a URL that gives the address of a resource and serves to locate the resource; but it can also include other components such as an XPointer which we'll discuss later.

The act of effecting a link or "making it happen" is called traversal. Because of the way browser software processes the links, XLink speaks about traversing a link rather than following it. One traverses an HTML link by clicking on it. When one clicks the mouse, the link changes color; and the browser retrieves the resource. The resource could replace the one in the browser window or the browser may open a new window or frame. In this scenario, one can talk about following a link because one goes from one document to another.

XLink extends HTML's linking capabilities by providing for automatic traversal of links. In addition to a user action, such as clicking on a displayed portion of a linking element to initiate a traversal, a program can control traversal. If a link can be traversed starting at more than one of its resources, it is known as a multidirectional link. We should note, however, that the ability to go back and forth in following a one-directional link, such as with the use of the Back button, does not make the link multidirectional. XLink also permits specifying multiple or grouped link locators as we'll see later.

Background

XLink builds on HTML, an international standard called HyTime (ISO 10744:1992), and an SGML application called the Text Encoding Initiative (TEI). XLink aims to provide a much more powerful range of options for linking than HTML does. In addition to the familiar "click and jump" type of link, XLink will also support new functions such as typed links, links with a specific role or behavior, two-way links (links that can be traversed just as easily in either direction), and multidirectional links (links that connect two or more targets.)

The XLink document defines a link as an "explicit relationship between two or more data objects or portions of data objects." In essence, a link is synonymous with linking element and includes the angle bracket symbols (< and >), the element name, and any attributes enclosed in the symbols. While HTML offers only a single type of link, XLink offers several possibilities. Links can be simple (inline) or extended (out-of-line.)

While HTML only recognizes two elements that can act as links, an XML link exists simply because the link element says it does. The element's attributes establish the link which means that, by giving it the right attributes, any XML element can act as a linking element. If attribute names conflict, one can re-map (redefine) the attributes to avoid collisions by using the xml:attributes attribute.

XLink uses the xml:link attribute as the primary attribute to identify an element as a link, as in the following example:

```
<A xml:link="simple" href="http://www.w3.org/">The W3C</A>
```

We must not forget that an element that is declared as a link element must also conform to the structure specified in the DTD.

Simple and Extended Links

XLink defines two types of linking element:

A simple link, which is usually inline and always one-directional and

A much more general extended link, which may be either inline or out-of-line and can be unidirectional or multi-directional. A multi-directional link points to more than one remote resource by separating the information about the local resource and that about the remote resources into separate elements. Multidirectional links, links originating from read-only resources, and so on, must be extended links.

Both kinds of links can have various types of information associated with them. This information, which is supplied in the form of attributes on linking elements, includes:

- Locators. A locator string identifies a participating resource; so each remote resource requires one or more locators to identify the remote resources participating in the link
- Semantics of the link which specify whether the link is inline or out-of-line and identify the role of the link to application software
- Semantics of the remote resources
- Semantics of the local resource. These last two items specify the role of the resource and identify to application software the part the resource plays in the link.

Every link is either inline or out-of-line. The inline status of a link is indicated with an attribute called inline. It can have the value true (the default) or false. If the link is inline, its content counts as a local resource of the link. (However, any locator subelements inside the linking element are not considered part of the local resource; they are simply part of the linking element machinery.) If the link is out-of-line, its content does not count as a local resource.

A simple inline link contains all the information about the link itself and both the local and remote resources encapsulated in the single href attribute of the linking element. It does not require an application to search for other elements for information about the locators. This is like the HTML A link that includes an HREF="URL" attribute.

Simple links are pretty much like the basic linking of HTML. HTML links are an all-or-nothing situation: either there's a link or there isn't. All the links are the same and have no way to describe the nature of the relationship between two linked resources.

Simple links can also support a limited amount of additional functionality. They have only one locator and thus, for convenience, combine the functions of a linking element and a locator into a single element. As a result of this combination, the simple linking element offers both a locator attribute and all the link and resource semantic attributes. Simple links can only be expressed using inline link syntax while extended links can use both inline and out-of-line syntax but usually the latter.

Because XML simple links are like HTML hyperlinks, they share the same problems. One of these problems is "link rot," the "link to nowhere"that points to a page or document that no longer exists.

Extended Links

An extended link differs from a simple link in that it "extends" the functionality of simple links by adding the ability to connect any number of resources. This gives XLink its power, as extended links provide the ability to establish bi-directional links. Extended links are more often out-of-line than simple links and do not even have to be physically contained in the document that uses them. They can also be used to:

- enable outgoing links in documents that cannot be modified to add an inline link, such as most multimedia formats in which the coding doesn't allow modification to embed links
- create links to and from resources that cannot contain the links themselves, such as formats with no native support for embedded links
- enable the dynamic filtering, addition, and modification of links on demand. This capability could allow experienced readers of a technical manual, for example, to modify the links at a certain point so they can take a different path than novice readers
- enable application software to process the links in a variety of other ways, according to its own needs
- link together any number of resources, resulting in multiple targets instead of a simple one-to-one relationship as in HTML
- enable other advanced hypermedia capabilities

Although an out-of-line simple link is meaningful, it is uncommon. Such a link is called "one-ended" and is typically used to associate discrete semantic properties with locations; but these properties are not considered full-fledged resources of the link. Most out-of-line links are extended links which offer a much wider range of uses.

When multiple resources participate in a link, as in extended links, semantics (the ability to describe a link) becomes critical. Otherwise, it would be meaningless to offer multiple locators without a sensible way of either describing the relationship, or, at the very least, distinguishing between two parallel resources.

In a simple link, it isn't important to define whether the attribute should be used to define local resources, remote resources, or both because a simple link combines the description of both local and remote resources into a single element. With extended links, however, the distinction between local and remote resources becomes more important.

Extended links separate the information about the local resource from that about the remote resource. Each extended link defined in the "local resource" element can have one or more child elements, each of which describes a different remote resource. Such a link, in simplified form without attributes, might look like this:

```
<localresource [local resource attributes]
              [link attributes]>
      <remoteresource {remote resource1 attributes]/>
      <remoteresource {remote resource2 attributes]/>
      <remoteresource {remote resource3 attributes]/>
</localresource>
```

In this case, the parent element, <localresource >, defines a link from the local resource to three separate remote resources, each with its own attributes (href="URL").

Examples

Elements implementing extended links do not need to be named Extended; they just need to have the xml:link attribute set to "extended". The following example shows how a single inline extended link rather than multiple simple ones could go from a book review to an online purchase order:

```
<distribextlink xml:link="extended"
      inline="true"
      title="Online Purchase Order">
      <distriblink xml:link="locator"
            href="http://amazon.com/orderform.html"
            title="Amazon.com"/>
      <distriblink xml:link="locator"
            href="http://barnesandnoble.com/orderform.html"
            title="Barnes & Noble"/>
      <distriblink xml:link="locator"
            href="http://borders.com/orderform.html"
            title="Borders Books"/>
      Buy a Copy</distribextlink>
```

In this example, the xml:link="extended" element defines the characteristics of the link and of the local resource (<distriblink>). The xml:link="locator" element defines the remote resources. Some of the attributes in this example, specifically inline and href, can apply to either the local resource or the remote one. Other attributes, such as the title, can be associated in different ways with both the local and the remote resource.

When the user drags the mouse cursor over the words "Buy a Copy," a pop-up window displays the value of the <distriblink> element's title attribute (Online Purchase Order). Then, when the user actuates the link by clicking on the words "Buy a Copy," a pop-up menu offers options to order from a variety of suppliers. In our example, these would be

Amazon.com
Barnes & Noble
Borders Books

The name of each supplier on the menu has its own href attribute pointing to the URL of the remote resource. Each resource also has its own title attribute that displays a different pop-up box when the mouse moves over the list of three distributors. The menu line immediately beneath the cursor would most likely be highlighted in some way to identify what the user is pointing at. Selecting one of the three suppliers would then open the URL of the remote resource.

The following example shows an out-of-line extended link for a commentary that includes links to an essay, a rebuttal, and a comparison:

```
<commentary xml:link="extended" inline="false">
<locator href="smith2.1" role="Essay"/>
<locator href="jones1.4" role="Rebuttal"/>
<locator href="robin3.2" role="Comparison"/>
</commentary>
```

An out-of-line link's definition does not have to be established at a specific point within a document. It can be established elsewhere in the document or out on the Web. Out-of-line links are also stored externally to the document. A key issue with out-of-line extended links is how linking application software can find and manage them, particularly when they are stored in completely separate documents from those in which their participating resources appear. XLink provides a mechanism called an extended link group element to identify relevant link-containing documents. The extended link group element allows storing the links as a group in one document and permits the user to activate them all at once. This could be useful to create an XML document that is made up only of fragments from several other documents. When a reader loads the document or clicks a link, that document or link will include all the fragments at one time. Out-of-line links can also serve to create collections of interlinked documents and to link the collections together.

Building Links

Building an XML link isn't exactly simple. It takes more than an href attribute for an element to be a link. The following sample declaration for a simple link shows all the possible XLink-related attributes it may have:

```
<!ELEMENT simple ANY>
<!ATTLIST simple
xml:link CDATA #FIXED "simple"
%locator.att;
%remote-resource-semantics.att;
%local-resource-semantics.att;
%simple-link-semantics.att;
>
```

This example shows that the content model has a value of ANY. This indicates that any content model or declared content is acceptable. Every significant XLink element in a valid document must still conform to the constraints expressed in its governing DTD. In practice, a simple link for a citation might look like this:

```
<mylink xml:link="simple" title="Citation"
href="http://www.xyz.com/xml/foo.xml" show="new"
content-role="Reference">as discussed in Smith(1997)</mylink>
```

The corresponding attribute-list declarations for the mylink element might look like this:

```
<!ELEMENT mylink (#PCDATA)>
<!ATTLIST mylink
xml:link            CDATA #FIXED "simple"
href                          CDATA #REQUIRED
content-role         CDATA #IMPLIED
>
```

Attributes and their meaning

The following simple link uses several attributes:

```
<reviewlink xml:link="simple"
      href=http://www.reviews.com/books.xml"
```

```
inline="true"
role="ReviewLink"
title="Link to review"
content-role="completereview"
content-title=FULL Review"
show="new"
actuate="user"
behavior="default">
```

The XLinking element (<reviewlink> in this case) usually only requires two attributes: the xml:link and href. All the others are optional; and some of the optional ones have default values.

xml:link="value" : The xml:link attribute is what marks an element as a linking element. The linking element must include this attribute regardless of whether it describes a local or remote resource. The value of this attribute can be simple, extended, locator, group, or document, depending on the type of link. In an ordinary extended link, the value of the attribute would be a "locator" which points to an actual target resource. The xml:link="group" attribute identifies the extended link as a link group rather than as an ordinary extended link which would have a value of "extended." We'll discuss extended link groups more in detail later. Using the xml:link="document"attribute, on the other hand, identifies the child elements of an extended link group.

If the DTD defines the value of the linking element's xml:link attribute, there is no need to supply it in the tag, as the DTD definition cannot be overridden. When used in a DTD, the information is stored in the attribute declaration. This reduces the size of the document and is more convenient to the document author who can define the purpose of the element in the DTD:

```
<!ATTLIST link xml:link CDATA #FIXED "simple"
               href     CDATA #REQUIRED>
<link href="..." >the link</link>
```

Whether supplied in the tag or in the DTD, this attribute must be entered somewhere to let the application know that this element is to be used for linking purposes.

Declaring the xml:link one time as a fixed value, as in the example above, and placing it in the DTD, avoids having to declare the attribute every time one wants to use an element. With the declaration out of the way, an XML <MYLINK> link begins to look just like an HTML hyperlink:

```
<MYLINK HREF="http://www.w3.org/">The W3C<MYLINK>
```

The placement of the declaration raises a technical issue. If the declaration resides in the main DTD (its external DTD subset), an XML client must download the whole DTD to find out about linking rules. This adds to the overhead and processing time. If, on the other hand, the declaration resides in the internal DTD subset contained in the document, this breaks SGML interoperability unless the internal DTD subset also includes declarations for the element's other attributes as well. That is because SGML specifies that each element can have only one attribute list declaration. The SGML standard will need to be modified to resolve this issue. Otherwise, a new mechanism will need to be developed to identify links to XML.

href="URL" : The href attribute serves the same function as it does in HTML: it identifies where to find the remote resource. XLink extends href by:

- Allowing any element type to indicate the existence of a link
- Defining the precise meaning of the fragment identifier (the part of the URL that follows the # or |) in cases when the target of the link is an XML document
- Providing links with human-readable labels
- Providing links with machine-readable labels
- Specifying policies for the context in which links are displayed and processed
- Specifying policies for when links are traversed
- Supporting extended linking groups
- Supporting multi-ended links

In HTML, the pound sign or hash symbol (#) preceding an identifier name serves to link to a specific element in the current file or in another file.

```
<link href="../myfiles/detail.xml#part3" See details, part 3</link>
```

This delivers the entire document to the browser. The reader then scrolls to the element with the given identifier name. XML uses the fragment identifier (#) in the same way if the target resource is an HTML document. However, if the target resource is an XML document, what follows the # sign must be an XPointer which we'll discuss later.

Inline="value" : The inline attribute has only two allowable values: "true," the default, and "false." If the local resource is inline, one need not include this attribute, as the default assumes that it is inline. However, if the local resource is out-of-line, one indicates this by specifying the value "false."

Role="value" : The optional role attribute can apply to either the local or remote resource or possibly to both in the case of extended links. It identifies the meaning of the link to the application software processing the document. To understand how this attribute might be useful, imagine a search engine capable of showing all links in a review document grouped by their roles. All links with the role="reviewlink" would appear at the top of the page, followed by other links which could be broken down further into separate sections. If we had additional role attributes such as photo or audio clips (role="photo" and role="audioclip"), we could further limit a search to those reviews that had a picture of the author or an audio clip of an interview with the author, for example.

title="value" : The optional title attribute, like role, can help define either local or remote resources or possibly both in the case of extended links. XML applications can decide whether to use this label and what to use it for. Because it follows the same concept as in HTML, it may well be used in a similar way, probably to provide a human-readable description of the link. It might appear as a pop-up hint within an XML browser when the mouse passes over the link. It differs from the role attribute which is intended for machine consumption.

content-role="value" : When a link is inline (the linking element is a resource of the link), a local resource can have a content-role attribute and a content-title attribute distinct from the title and role attributes. That is because a simple link already uses the title and role attributes to provide the processing application with information about the simple element's position in this link and has nowhere else to put information about the target resource.

The role attribute provides information about the link – the relationship between the two or more resources defined by the link. The content-role attribute, on the other hand, provides information about the specific resource being pointed to. It identifies the part that the resource plays in the link. It will probably be used primarily for processing by software. This attribute can be used only in an element which defines a local resource. In other words, it describes a remote resource in the context of the local resource.

For example, in a thesaurus application, this attribute might serve to extend the attribute list for the broad-term element. The content-role attribute could indicate that the current term is a narrower term (NT) of the broad term to which it is linked:

```
<!ATTLIST broad-term
    xml-link        CDATA      #FIXED "SIMPLE"
    role            CDATA      #FIXED "BT"
    content-role    CDATA      #FIXED "NT"
    href            CDATA      #REQUIRED
```

content-title="value" : The content-title attribute is used only in elements defining a local resource; but we don't really know what it will be good for until application software is developed to take advantage of it. Since the content-role attribute is intended primarily for use by application software, content-title might be used primarily for human consumption and may act as a caption to explain to users the part the resource plays in the link and to translate the information provided in content-role for human understanding. It may also display like a "tool tip" when the mouse passes over it, rather than or in addition to the link title.

show="value" : The show attribute introduces an improved level of functionality over HTML by formalizing the behavior of all links, rather than relying on a link with a particular name, such as HTML's IMG element. This optional attribute appears only in elements describing remote resources and tells the application software how to display the retrieved resource. Here, display does not mean the same thing as in HTML. It does not refer to the type face, fonts, point size, etc. Rather, it refers to the window or other context in which the linking element itself appears.

The show attribute has three possible values: replace (the default), new, and embed. The replace value works just like the default Web browser. When one clicks on the link, the browser retrieves it and replaces the contents of the current window with the contents of the target.

The show="new" attribute opens a new window to display the target resource, leaving the original window on the screen. This approach could be used to display elements that refer to multimedia, such as graphics or video files, where the media would appear in its own window. It could also serve to display small comments or annotations or to support help functions. Whatever is done to the target resource doesn't affect the display of the starting resource. Thus, a piece of text from an external document can be retrieved without its style declarations affecting the current document. The disadvantage of this approach is that the user must explicitly close the window to return to the original display. Leaving many such windows open could impair system performance and eventually consume all available RAM.

Specifying show="embed" tells the processor that when the XLink is traversed, it should insert the target resource's contents into the linking resource at the point where the traversal started. However the XLink specification doesn't make clear exactly where that will be in relation to the content of the element containing the simple link.

The show attribute allows an author to create virtual documents composed of fragments of other documents. One can also create dynamic tables of contents and indices by picking up parts of other elements and virtually copying them to the link location. Whenever a reader passes the cursor over a reference note (footnote or endnote) with embedded links, the browser could insert the full citation or an abstract at the point where the reference note occurs.

An author can declare a default show attribute value for an extended link element that will then override any default values declared for the locator elements in the DTD. For example, in the following example, the first location element has the default show attribute value of replace; but the second location element has a show attribute value of new that overrides the default definition:

```
<extended show="replace">
    <location href="mypage.html"/>
    <location href="hispage.htm" show="new"/>
</extended>
```

actuate="value" : The actuate attribute, as the name implies, makes something happen. In XLink, an element which describes a remote resource can have a link in the document that remains inactive until it is traversed. It can have either of two values: user or auto. Actuate="user" is the default setting and need not be explicitly specified. This means that the user decides when to traverse the link. The traversal will usually occur by clicking on the link.

However, if the value is set to auto, link traversal occurs automatically as soon as it is encountered, without any user intervention. Reading the link and fetching its target resource are considered part of the process of reading the current resource. This can be very powerful, especially when used in conjunction with show="embed."This allows authors to create new documents, on-the-fly, made up entirely of chunks of other documents or fragments mixed in with one's own content.

This collection of documents and document fragments evokes copyright and other legal issues as well as some technical problems that need to be ironed out. When a document or document fragment gets included in a main document, does the included portion display in the same style – fonts, colors, etc. – as the main document? What happens if the linked resource also has show="embed" or actuate="auto" links? Do all these links and the ones they link to get inserted into the main document?

behavior="value" : The optional behavior attribute can only be used in elements which describe a remote resource. It describes the link as a whole – the connection between the source and the target. One can enter any value at this point; but what one enters here depends on what the application that will use this data can do with it. In other words, the processing capabilities of the application will determine the value of this attribute. If there is no application to make use of this attribute or if the application does not understand the value, whatever one enters here will be ignored. Possible applications might be to extract quotes to include in the text of the linking resource or to implement a variety of transition effects, such as fade-in, wipe, or dissolve, when displaying graphics or film clips.

Remapping

Sometimes attribute names could easily be used for other purposes, resulting in potential conflicts. XLink allows attribute remapping through the xml:attributes attribute. This lets authors change significant attributes for linking within XML. The process uses pairs of names. In each pair, the first name is one of the default XLink names (role, href, title, show, inline, content-role, content-title, actuate, behavior, steps). The second name specifies the attribute that will be treated as though it were playing the role assigned to the first.

```
<!ATTLIST person-link
     role            CDATA #IMPLIED
     xml:link        CDATA #FIXED "SIMPLE"
     link-role       CDATA #IMPLIED
     xml:attributes CDATA #FIXED "role link-role">
```

This example uses both role and link-role attributes. It maps the role attribute to the link-role attribute for the person-link element. This allows the person-link element to take the following form:

```
<person-link role="parent" link-role="footnote">
```

This allows a person (role="parent") to play a different role than a link (link-role="footnote"). This distinguishes between two different meanings of the word "parent." It is important to remember that XLink does not permit using any attributes beginning with xml when remapping attributes. While it might be tempting to remap the role attribute to xml-role, it would be wrong.

Extended Link Group

When links reside outside a document, it can become difficult to manage them. An XML document may not always "know" which other documents share links with it, especially if those links are stored in content generated and managed by other people. XLink addresses the challenge of managing the mazes of links by offering the possibility of centralizing linking information and including several locations in a link through the xml:link attribute which can create extended link groups that help to manage links.

An extended link group element is a special kind of extended link that may be used to store a list of links to other documents that together constitute an interlinked group. Each such document is identified by means of an extended link document element, a special kind of locator element. The extended link group element really doesn't point or link to anywhere at all. It simply groups together several locator elements that together form an extended link that might look something like:

```
<extended>
<locator.../>
<locator.../>
</extended>
```

When an application encounters an extended link group in an XML document, it tries to locate the resources. These resources are identified in the child elements that have xml:link attributes with a value of "document." When the application finds those resources, it looks for any extended link groups that they contain. If it finds any, it then adds the corresponding remote resources to the menu of available links.

Any extended link groups that point back to the original document establish "bi-directional" links that allow a reader to return to the original document. If the application has enough "intelligence," it could retain this bi-directional link across sessions, along with all the other links. These bi-directional links could then constitute a sort of virtual history list, making all of the related links always present and possibly obviating the need for a Back button.

Multidirectional links that can be traversed in either direction can bring up a list of links that include the document from which the user came by clicking on the target document or just using its linking interface. They could also allow simultaneous updating of the content that appears in multiple frames by selecting a single link in a document.

Extended link groups can tell documents to check each other for relevant links and allow the creation of centralized links for sets of related data. They offer the user or processing application a set of choices from a link rather than a single target. An extended link's set of choices might appear as a pop-up menu or other interface that lets the user select an option. For example, in a thesaurus, a user could click on a word to see a set of synonyms in a pop-up window. Selecting a word could then lead to further information about it.

Extended link groups enable several documents to share a common "menu" of links. This makes it easier to maintain the menu because one can add a new link to the extended link group which becomes immediately available to all documents that use the extended link group. This added flexibility will give power users a great new tool for navigation; but it will confuse many who already get lost in the web of HTML links.

Extended link groups require creating two elements: one to define a group and the other to identify the documents in the group. The following sample declarations for extended link group and extended link document elements show all the possible XLink-related attributes they may have. The xml:link attribute value for an extended link group element must be group; and the value for an extended link document element must be document.

```
<!ELEMENT group (document*)>
<!ATTLIST group
xml:link      CDATA #FIXED "group"
steps     CDATA #IMPLIED
>

<!ELEMENT document EMPTY>
<!ATTLIST document
xml:link CDATA #FIXED "document"
%locator.att;
>
```

There are situations wherein an extended link group directs the application software to locate another document which contains an extended link group of its own. While there might be occasions when processing several levels of extended link groups could be useful, there is a potential for infinite iterations, such as when an extended link group points back to the original document or to a document containing yet another extended link group. This repetition could result in infinite links and link loops. Multiple layers of multidirectional links could try a reader's patience as the network bogs down, churning its way through the endless chain of links.

An author can prevent such a vicious circle from happening by using the steps attribute (steps="n"). The number specified in the steps attribute indicates how many layers of nesting the author wants to allow or how far down the chain to proceed before stopping the search for further extended links. Specifying steps="2" tells the application to go to the indicated resource(s) (one step), then to any resources named in extended link groups in the indicated resource(s) (second steps). Then the application should stop.

The steps attribute does not have any normative effect, though. This means that XLink does not require an application to obey this attribute. However, we can hope that the more user-friendly software packages will obey it.

XPointer

XLink governs how links are created and managed in XML. But XML adds some new functionality that accommodates linking to fragments of documents.

This is done through XPointer (an abbreviation for eXtended Pointer). XPointer defines a language which is expected to be used with XLink. It "builds upon the XML Path Language (XPath) to support addressing into the internal structures of XML documents." It also defines the constructs that support such addressing. In particular, it provides for specific reference to elements, character strings, and other parts of XML documents, whether or not they bear an explicit ID attribute; using traversals of a document's structure; and choice of parts based on their properties such as element types, attribute values, character content, and relative position, containment, and order. XLink directs how to insert links into an XML document to point to something like another document or an image. XPointer, on the other hand, defines the meaning of the fragment identifier that goes on a URL when linking to an XML document, MIME media type, "text/xml" or "application/xml."

XPointer uses XPath as its common expression language and extends it to allow its use for addressing ranges as well as nodes, for locating information by string matching, and for using addressing expressions in URIs as fragment identifiers. XPointer expressions locate information by navigating through a document's structure to select parts based on properties such as element types, attribute values, character content, and relative position and order.

The locator for a resource is typically provided by means of a Uniform Resource Identifier Reference, or URI Reference. XPointers can be used as fragment identifiers to specify a more precise sub-resource. (We'll discuss fragment identifiers more in detail in the next section.) XPointers can be used with URI References other than those associated with hypertext links, such as in system identifiers for XML external entities. XPointer governs fragment identifiers that point into an XML resource. It has no control over the syntax or semantics of a locator that identifies a resource that is not an XML document, such as an HTML or PDF document.

XPointers operate on the XML Information Set, a tree derived from the elements and other markup constructs of an XML document. This is the same tree that XSL patterns and XPath expressions use. XPointers operate by selecting particular parts of such trees, often by their structural relationship to other identified nodes (such as a nearby node bearing an ID). XPointers can be repeated because they can express multiple selections with each one operating on what the prior one finds.

If an XPointer contains more than one locator, the locators are separated by two periods (..). The XPointer then refers to all the content beginning with the element identified by the first locator and ending with the element identified by the last locator.

Fragment Identifiers

XPointer's most powerful use is to retrieve fragments of text or data contained inside XML resources. HTML also allows a URL to contain a fragment identifier as in the following example:

HREF="URL#FragmentIdentifier"

XML can use HTML's fragment identifier notation to link from XML documents to any non-XML resource, such as image files, HTML pages, Java applets, and so on, just as HTML does. However, XML can do many more interesting and useful things when that resource is an XML document. Even in simple links, it can let authors and developers treat elements as the primary unit involved in linking rather than entire documents. Because XML's addressing strategy is interoperable with HTML's, an author can use its special addressing in HTML pages to address parts of XML documents. XPointer's syntax for locating items is considerably more robust than HTML's though. It provides a number of tools that can address parts of documents by structure, ID, HTML anchor, or even text content.

As XML's href attribute is designed to be interoperable with HTML, it uses a similar, but more powerful, syntax for fragment identifiers. HTML uses a URL, optionally followed by a question mark (?) and a query to effect a search. It uses a pound sign or hash mark (#) followed by a fragment identifier to locate a document fragment. XPointer uses a similar syntax which would look something like this:

href="URL#XPointer"

or

href="URL|XPointer"

The # in the first example retrieves the whole document referenced by the URL. The client then has to locate the fragment itself, as is the case for the # fragments in HTML links. If the show attribute is set to "replace," the processor substitutes the referenced document for the current one. If the fragment identifier refers to a named part of another document, a reader might infer that the rest of the document is not important and that it would be a waste of bandwidth to receive it all. The following example links to Some College's online catalog for chemistry courses:

http://www.somecollege.edu/catalog.html#chemistry

This URL tells the browser to go to Some College's catalog.html document and go to the chemistry section which should have a tag like <a name="chemistry">. After locating the tag, the browser displays the document beginning with the Chemistry section.

If the target document does not have an <a name="name" > tag, the browser will try its best to locate the intended document. It will pretend that the document does not contain the fragment identifier; and it will open the document at the beginning. This will not present a significant problem if the same person or organization maintains all the documents and the linked documents they refer to. However, if the document has no <a name="name"> tags or if the browser cannot determine the name values or if the portion to link to does not have a name, the fragment identifier will not work.

XPointer introduces a new "connector" symbol for use in an href URL attribute. The "pipe" or "vertical bar symbol" (|) is used in the second example above instead of the pound sign or hash symbol to indicate that the processor should retrieve only the referenced part of the document. The pipe symbol lets the server software interpret what to do with the information that follows the |. For documents, this would usually mean retrieving a portion of text. If the target resource were a streaming media file, for example, the software which processes the file might specify where to begin playing the file and for how long. For example, the following statement:

```
href="author.mov|start=10sec,dur=25sec"
```

would play 25 seconds of a QuickTime video of an author interview starting 10 seconds from the beginning of the clip.

Addressing

XPointer extends the XPath syntax for locating data portions to permit addressing non-node locations, such as user selections, and to specify how to use such locators as XML fragment identifiers. It does not specify what an application should do with those locations, however. XPointer does not require the implementation of traversal to a resource, for example. It lets the application control user traversal. So, traversal in a formatted-text browser might scroll to and highlight the designated location. A structure-oriented graphical tree viewer or a document-relationship display might perform traversal in quite a different way. A search application, parser, archival system, or expert agent might use XPointers for other purposes entirely.

XPointer provides three ways for locators to retrieve resources: absolute and relative addressing and string-matching. Absolute location terms identify elements using the more conventional ID and NAME addressing schemes and some other basic locations. Relative terms allow links to refer to a resource by its position within the element tree of a document or even by its content. String-matching terms are the most limited; but they are more precise than the other techniques.

Absolute Keywords

Each XPointer keyword includes a set of empty parentheses to keep them consistent with other addressing keywords and to help ensure that the software (or human reader) will not get confused if the XPointer just happens to contain these words without parentheses. The default absolute keyword is root(). It is equivalent to using no fragment identifier at all, as it specifies and locates the root element of the entire resource as if it were a fragment. It also locates any adjacent processing instructions and/or other nodes permitted by XML. If an XPointer has no leading absolute location step (that is, it consists only of a RelPath), it is equivalent to having a leading / since the context node in the expression evaluation context is initialized to the root.

The id() keyword locates an element in a resource by its declared value and name. XML restricts the range of characters allowed in names and defines the contents as case-sensitive. For example, xptr(id("intro")) will retrieve the URI fragment identifier “intro”.

Relative Addressing

Using an ID is the easiest, most reliable way to locate a sub-resource of a given XML document. However, its use requires that an element include an id attribute and that one knows the id's value. XML supports a few special address mechanisms for use when one does not have an absolute address or if an absolute address cannot be used, regardless of whether the document contains any ID values. They can be used in an absolute address, although they are of most use in a relative addressing scheme. They are particularly useful when one needs to link to resources that one has no control over and, therefore, cannot set ID values for those resources. These methods just require one to know something about the structure of the target document.

The use of a relative location term presupposes a starting point (a location source). The relative location term then allows one to move around the target XML document by describing a location in relation to one’s location at that moment. If we compare document addressing to following directions in a city, an absolute address would identify a known landmark, such as Grand Central Station or the corner of Hollywood and Vine. A relative address would begin with an absolute address and give further directions such as:

go to the corner of Hollywood and Vine;

go west eight blocks;
the Guinness World of Records Museum will be on the left.

Each step of the instructions in a relative address depends on the correct execution of the previous step. After one mistake, the instructions just get one lost. If one goes north instead of west, one needs to stop for further directions. Relative addresses in XML operate the same way.

The origin() function enables addressing relative to out-of-line links as defined in XLink. The origin() keyword means "the place where you currently are" (not "the place where you started"). It lets a reader examine each part of a document in sequence, moving forward and backward at will. For example, one can point to the next chapter by saying something like "origin()+1" or to the previous chapter by saying "origin()-1". [That's not the real syntax but just an idea of how it's used.]

This method provides a meaningful context node list for any following location steps only if the XPointer is being processed by application software in response to a user request for traversal, for example as defined in the XLink specification. In that case, origin() locates the sub-resource from which the user initiated traversal. This allows XPointers to be used in applications to express relative locations when links do not reside directly at one of their endpoints. It is an error to use origin() when a locator provides a URI and it identifies a containing resource different from the resource from which traversal was initiated. It is also an error to use this function in a situation where user traversal is not occurring. This means that the origin() keyword can be used only to point to target resources that are in the document containing the link itself.

In addition to locating a document with the origin function, one can use here, and a variety of relationships, such as child, descendant, ancestor, preceding, following, psibling, and fsibling. The here() function enables locating the node for the element directly containing (as text) or bearing (as an attribute) the XPointer. It is especially useful for representing reusable relative links when the links reside directly at one of their endpoints, such as "the containing chapter". It also allows an XPointer to specify content "2 paragraphs below the link element," for example.

The following are the relative term keywords that XPointer allows. Each term consists of a keyword, followed by one or more steps that gets closer to the final location of the link resource:

child: selects the child element of the location source (must be elements nested directly under the source)
descendant: selects the elements that appear within the content of the location source (may be nested more than one level)

ancestor: selects the elements in whose content the location source is found (parent elements)
preceding: selects elements that appear before the location source
following: selects elements that appear after the location source
psibling: selects the preceding sibling elements of the location source (sibling elements share the same parent element)
fsibling: selects the following sibling elements of the location source (sibling elements share the same parent element)

Each of these keywords use the same set of arguments, enclosed in parentheses: (Instance, ElType, Attr, Value). They allow finding the attribute by name and value, similarly to id(). These keywords are useful when different element types declare like-named attributes and only some of them are IDs. Since a given id value may also appear as the value of many non-id attributes (especially idrefs) in a document, using name or value alone may not suffice.

The following statement selects the year that The Laughing Cow was first released:

```
laughcow.xml#child(1,releaseyear)
```

This example uses the child keyword which says, "Look at the immediate descendants of the location source." The values in parentheses ("1" and "releaseyear") further specify that child keyword by saying, "Look for the first child of the location source whose element name is 'releaseyear.'" A fuller, more complicated way of stating the same thing would be:

```
laughcow.xml#root().child(1,releaseyear)
```

Since the root() keyword is the default, it can be omitted from the statement, as in the first example. We should note that the second example has a period between the root() and child keywords. The period separates each succeeding address from the previous one because XPointer allows stringing addresses together. Each additional term changes the location source for whatever appears later on in the Xpointer.

Thus, a statement like:

```
laughcow.xml#child(1,cast).child(1,leadcast).child(2,male)
```

could locate the name of the second male lead. In essence, it says, "Locate the first child element of the location source named cast, then locate that cast element's first child element named leadcast, and finally, extract that leadcast element's second element named male." The first child keyword narrows the location source to the first cast child of root (which is implied), and so on.

String Matching

Absolute and relative location terms select complete elements. String location terms, on the other hand, can retrieve select text located within an element. They are extremely useful when one wants to link into non-XML data, such as text files, or into XML data that contains large blocks of text. String location terms take the following four arguments:

1. A number that indicates which occurrence of the specified string is required. One can use the keyword “all” to select all the occurrences.

2. The character string, enclosed in single or double quotes. One can specify a number to identify a particular character instead of a string.

3. A position number that indicates how many characters to count forward from the start of the matched string to locate the actual string required. If one doesn’t specify a value, the parser assumes a value of 1, as a value of 0 is not allowed. A positive number (for example, +2) counts from the left end of the string to the right. A negative value (-4) counts backward (to the left) from the right end of the string.

4. A number that indicates the number of characters in the string to be selected (its length). Not specifying a value or specifying 0 locates the position immediately before the character indicated by the position number. One can use an empty string, identified by a pair of quotes ("") to specify the point just after the character string to match.

String location terms might be used something like the following:

> string(3, "the",1,2) which selects the characters "he" from the third occurrence of the word "the".

If one has already selected the word, string(2," ") indicates the point between the character "t" and "h" in the word "the".

> string(1,"amazing",-6,3) selects the characters "maz" from the first occurence of the word "amazing".

Interactive Pointers

User selection in most user interfaces provides an everyday example of data portions that are seldom elements. The most common link-creation interface is to let the user select, and then make an XPointer that locates it, perhaps then using it in a hyperlink. To support even this simple case, XPointer must provide the ability to express non-node locations.

It is impossible to guarantee that links to target resources will never break. XLink and XPointer will not eliminate all "404 Document not found" errors. The resources could be changed enough that even the most robust link will break; or the resource could be deleted entirely. This creates a new variation of an old problem. A browser might locate a document but not a specific sub-resource in the document. An author could rewrite a link to add or remove elements or discuss another subject entirely. This could make all links irrelevant, even if they refer to resources using IDs. However, under typical conditions, XPointers can be made reasonably robust, particularly if they use relative addresses because they're more likely to retrieve something, even though a sub-resource may have changed or moved.

Experienced Web users will be familiar with an optional part of a URL which appears at the end of the URL, separated from it by a question mark (?). This device serves to pass information to a server such as search terms or data from fields in a form. XLink continues to support this URL option but suggests that vendors of "XML-aware" server software and database products use the xptr keyword to introduce a portion of a URL which queries a database, passes data to a CGI program, and so on. A URL employing this device might look something like the following:

```
href://[system name, path, file]?xptr=value
```

The value in this expression would be either an XPointer or a standard HTML name. The xptr keyword, then, links to another location in the current document or one in an external document.

Other node types

XPointer permits pointing to other kinds of markup, besides elements. These markup types include the contents of comments and processing instructions, but not entity and other declarations. A typical application, like a browser that uses XML coding, does not need all the physical markup (CDATA sections, comments, elements, PIs, and so on) that does not contribute to the document's structure. It is only interested in the parsed character content, the elements and attributes which form the logical markup.

When we address a document fragment using a URL, we usually refer to the logical markup. A hyperlink to a comment or processing instruction, for example, would not be very useful because the browser does not display the content of this markup in the normal browser window. One needs to select "View Source" to do this. However, users may find that information very important or they may need to use an XML document for something other than browsing. For example, they may need to edit it using an XML authoring tool or to feed it to another application to transform the XML into something else, such as database records for mail merge, for example. Consequently, XPointer allows addressing based on physical markup, even though most XML parsers currently available do not pass it to the applications such as browsers.

XPath

XPointer uses XPath as the language to address parts of an XML document. XPath's primary purpose is to address parts of an XML document by providing basic facilities for manipulation of strings, numbers and booleans (true/false statements). It uses a compact, non-XML syntax and operates on the abstract, logical structure of an XML document, rather than on its surface syntax. XPath models an XML document as a tree of nodes and gets its name from its use of a path notation as in URLs for navigating through the hierarchical structure of an XML document. In addition to its use for addressing, XPath is also designed so that it has a natural subset that can be used for matching (testing whether or not a node matches a pattern).

Node Types

XPath models an XML document as a tree of nodes. There are seven different types of node. They include root nodes, element nodes, attribute nodes, text nodes, processing instruction nodes, comment nodes, and namespace nodes. Some types of node also have an expanded-name, which is a pair consisting of a local part and a namespace URI. The local part is a string. The namespace URI is either null or a string that can have a fragment identifier. XPath defines a way to compute a string-value for each type of node.

XPath's main syntactic element is called an expression (expr) that can consist of four basic types:

- node-set (an unordered collection of nodes without duplicates)
- boolean (true or false)
- number (a floating-point number)
- string (a sequence of UCS characters)

Expression evaluation occurs with respect to a context which is determined by XSLT and XPointer. The context consists of:

- a node (the context node)
- a pair of non-zero positive integers (the context position and the context size)
- a set of variable bindings
- a function library

- the set of namespace declarations in scope for the expression

XPath expressions often occur in XML attributes. When this occurs, the grammar must be normalized. So, for example, if the grammar uses the character <, this must not appear in the XML source as < but must be quoted according to XML 1.0 rules by entering it as <. Within expressions, literal strings are delimited by single or double quotation marks, which are also used to delimit XML attributes. To avoid a quotation mark in an expression being interpreted by the XML processor as terminating the attribute value, the quotation mark can be entered as a character reference (" or '). Alternatively, the expression can use single quotation marks if the XML attribute is delimited with double quotation marks or vice-versa.

Location Path

One important kind of expression, and a special case of an expr, is the location path. Location paths are not the most general grammatical construct; but they are the most important ones. A location path selects a set of nodes relative to the context node. The result of evaluating an expression that is a location path is the node-set containing the nodes selected by the location path. An XPath LocationPath typically consists of a list of location steps separated by a slash (/). It is expressed in the form:

axis-name :: node-test[predicate]*

The axis-name specifies the tree relationship between the nodes selected by the location step and the context node. A double colon (::) separates the axis name from the node-test which specifies the node type and expanded-name of the nodes selected by the location step. After the node-test comes the predicate which consists of zero or more expressions, each in square brackets. The predicate further refines the set of nodes selected by the location step.

For example, in child::para[position()=1], child is the name of the axis, para is the node test, and [position()=1] is a predicate. The following expression would locate all the children of the context node that are of element type "List":

child::List

Some of the location paths and their syntax include:

- child::para selects the para element children of the context node
- child::* selects all element children of the context node
- child::text() selects all text node children of the context node

- child::node() selects all the children of the context node, whatever their node type
- attribute::name selects the name attribute of the context node
- attribute::* selects all the attributes of the context node
- descendant::para selects the para element descendants of the context node
- ancestor::div selects all div ancestors of the context node
- ancestor-or-self::div selects the div ancestors of the context node and, if the context node is a div element, the context node as well
- descendant-or-self::para selects the para element descendants of the context node and, if the context node is a para element, the context node as well
- self::para selects the context node if it is a para element. Otherwise, it selects nothing
- child::chapter/descendant::para selects the para element descendants of the chapter element children of the context node
- child::*/child::para selects all para grandchildren of the context node
- / selects the document root (which is always the parent of the document element)
- /descendant::para selects all the para elements in the same document as the context node
- /descendant::olist/child::item selects all the item elements in the same document as the context node that have an olist parent
- child::para[position()=1] selects the first para child of the context node
- child::para[position()=last()] selects the last para child of the context node
- child::para[position()=last()-1] selects the last but one para child of the context node
- child::para[position()>1] selects all the para children of the context node other than the first para child of the context node

- following-sibling::chapter[position()=1] selects the next chapter sibling of the context node

- preceding-sibling::chapter[position()=1] selects the previous chapter sibling of the context node

- /descendant::figure[position()=42] selects the forty-second figure element in the document

- /child::doc/child::chapter[position()=5]/child::section[position()=2] selects the second section of the fifth chapter of the doc document element

- child::para[attribute::type="warning"] selects all para children of the context node that have a type attribute with a value of warning

- child::para[attribute::type='warning'][position()=5] selects the fifth para child of the context node that has a type attribute with a value of warning

- child::para[position()=5][attribute::type="warning"] selects the fifth para child of the context node if that child has a type attribute with a value of warning

- child::chapter[child::title='Introduction'] selects the chapter children of the context node that have one or more title children with string-value equal to Introduction

- child::chapter[child::title] selects the chapter children of the context node that have one or more title children

- child::*[self::chapter or self::appendix] selects the chapter and appendix children of the context node

- child::*[self::chapter or self::appendix][position()=last()] selects the last chapter or appendix child of the context node

Absolute and Relative Location Paths

There are two kinds of location path: relative location paths and absolute location paths. A relative location path consists of a sequence of one or more location steps separated by a forward slash mark (/). The steps in a relative location path are composed together from left to right. Each step in turn selects a set of nodes relative to a context node. An initial sequence of steps is composed together with a following step as follows. The initial sequence of steps selects a set of nodes relative to a context node. Each node in that set is used as a context node for the following step. The sets of nodes identified by the second step are joined together. The set of nodes identified by the composition of the steps is this union. For example, child::div/child::para selects the para element children of the div element children of the context node, or, in other words, the para element grandchildren that have div parents.

XPath provides absolute addresses as well, using an initial / to locate the document root, and id() to locate the node with a given XML id value. An absolute location path may have a relative location path following the / whereas a / by itself selects the root node of the document containing the context node. If it is followed by a relative location path, then the location path selects the set of nodes that would be selected by the relative location path relative to the root node of the document containing the context node.

The XPath draft uses the slash (/) as the delimiter between location steps. It also defines the double slash (//) as an abbreviation for the descendants axis, causing some servers to change occurrences of // to / in fragment identifiers. This problem is under examination to determine its severity.

Navigation

XPointer often uses steps to navigate within the tree. XPath provides the fundamental navigation directions that have corresponding relationships called axes. These relative axes are ordered by their distance from the "context node." Thus, axes such as ancestor and preceding consider nodes in reverse document order. If no context node list is explicitly provided, the context is the root element of the containing resource.

XPath's relative axes are:

child: Locates direct child nodes of the context node. Unless restricted by a predicate, children of all types (element, processing instruction, comment, and text) are located. Attributes are not considered children of the elements that bear them. (The attribute axis serves to locate attributes.)

descendant: Locates nodes appearing anywhere within the content of the context node.

descendant-or-self: Identical to the descendant axis except that the context node itself is included as a candidate,.preceding all descendants.

parent: Locates the element nodes directly containing the context node.

ancestor: Locates element nodes containing the context node (since only elements properly have children as defined here). The first node in the list is the immediate parent of the context node, the last node in the list is root().

ancestor-or-self: Identical to the ancestor axis except that the context node itself is included as a candidate, preceding all ancestors.

preceding-sibling: Locates sibling nodes (nodes that share the same parent as the context node) that appear before (preceding) the context node. The nodes are considered in reverse document order, so that the first node in the list is the immediately preceding sibling, and the last node in the list is the first child of the parent.

following-sibling: Locates sibling nodes (sharing their parent with the context node) that appear after (following) the context node. The nodes in the list appear in document order.

preceding: Locates nodes that begin before (preceding) the entire context node. The list is in reverse document order: the node closest to the context node first, root() last. Ancestors are included.

following: Locates nodes that begin after (following) the entire context node. The list is in document order: the first node in the list is for the first node whose start-tag occurs after the context node's end-tag; no ancestors are included.

self: Locates (for each context node in the context node list), a singleton nodelist containing that same context node. This is useful for applying multiple predicates to a single axis, particular when predicates other than the first one must test a context node's position among all the context nodes that were selected by the prior predicates.

attribute: The attributes of the context node. The order of nodes on this axis is undefined. Typically, a single attribute will be selected by name.

This brief look at XPath considered how it models an XML document as a tree of nodes and operates on the logical structure of an XML document. We discussed some of XPath's syntax and showed how it differs from that of the rest of XML. We identified the expression as its main syntactic element; and we considered the location path as the most important type of expression. We looked at absolute and relative location paths and identified the relationships that XPath uses for navigation. While some of this is quite technical, it is not meant to make the reader a programmer or an expert in using XPath. Rather, it aims to help a user understand the syntax and constructs when one encounters them in the use of XSL, XLink, and XPointer.

This chapter began with an overview of XLink, XPointer, and XPath and focused primarily on XLink and XPointer. It discussed HTML links insofar as they help us to understand XML links. It examined the differences between simple and extended links and how links are built. It covered the various attributes and their meanings and looked at remapping attributes to avoid conflicts as well as the use of extended link groups. We then went on to examine XPointer which permits retrieval of resources that are contained within XML documents. We examined how to identify and link to document fragments. We discussed the three ways to address a link (absolute keywords, relative keywords, and string matching) as well as the use of interactive pointers.

Now that we understand the various parts of XML and how they work, we can proceed to study how a parser uses XML markup to process and manipulate the information content.

Chapter 5

Processing XML Data

HTML's principal function is for document layout and display. It does not understand the components of a document and, therefore, cannot do anything with them. The value of XML, on the other hand, is that it understands the structure and meaning of the data elements in a document and allows processing that data. Thus, XML documents interact with software, whether a word processor, text editor, page layout program, database, spreadsheet, or other type of application.

The XML processing software is called a parser. Basically, a parser just interprets the text or data. Software filters included in the parser allow manipulation of that data for the intended recipient, whether that recipient is a human reader or a software application. In fact, XML's greatest benefits may be in communication between computers and between computers and other devices.

In this chapter, we shall look at some of the ways XML can manipulate data and possible reasons for doing so. We shall then proceed to examine the two different approaches that an XML processor can follow. Each approach has its corresponding Application Programming Interface (API). Event-driven processing uses the Simple API for XML (SAX) while the tree-manipulation method uses the Document Object Model (DOM). We shall discuss these two approaches and their corresponding APIs and conclude by considering some of the applications that XML can help to implement.

Data Manipulation

An author might need to write programs to process XML for a variety of reasons, such as for delivery to multiple media; delivery to multiple target groups; adding, removing, and restructuring information; database loading; and reporting.

Delivery to Multiple Media

Authors may want to publish information in different media such as in hard copy, CD-ROM, on the Web, etc. For example, if they choose to publish on the Web, they will most likely select HTML which will remain the Internet's language for the foreseeable future. However, selection of HTML version 4 may not operate the same as version 3.2 on some browsers. Selecting DHTML (Dynamic HTML) introduces another wrinkle: whose flavor to use: Microsoft's or Netscape's.

Authors could rely on using only those HTML tags supported by all browsers (the common denominator approach), optimize HTML pages for use on specific browsers, or include scripts in the HTML pages to generate browser-specific code. XML could permit checking the type and version of the browser and transforming the XML data on-the-fly to the most appropriate version of HTML. The advantage is that XML allows an author to manage a single source file. Any formatting and data processing occurs separate from the data; so, when a new version of a software program appears, it may require a new conversion program; but the data will not have to be modified.

Delivery to Multiple Target Groups

Sometimes information needs to be presented differently to different types of groups. For example, library patrons don't need all the detailed information that library staff require. Novice searchers need more help and prompts than advanced and expert searchers. People associated with an institution, such as a college or university, will have a wider variety of information tools available when accessing a library catalog than the general public accessing the same catalog remotely.

XML allows one to customize the viewable information to a particular user group. For example, an experienced searcher does not need to see all the prompts and help screens that a beginning searcher does. Similarly, when one visits a site frequently, it would be nice to have the site "remember" what has been examined and what one has done on previous visits. A visitor could have a customized display that reflects previous activity and creates bookmarks to return to the location of the last visit, rather than having to retrace his or her steps each time.

XML can become a portable interchange format that will find its way into many software products. It facilitates the transfer of data between systems by providing a universal format for files in transit. Interoperability will most likely be accomplished through the use of schemas which we'll discuss in more detail in chapter 7. While some applications will use XML as a native format, most will probably incorporate it as an import/export format and maintain proprietary internal formats. This will require constant translation between the proprietary and XML formats.

Adding, Removing, And Restructuring Information

XML and XSL contain facilities for doing calculations, testing conditions, and performing other functions. One can build complex instructions to process individual elements or even characters within an XML document. One can also arrange the data generated from a database as desired when defining a report. This could involve leaving data out or computing new data based on existing ones (e.g. totals, averages, etc.)

For example, consider the following example of a purchase request for a book:

```
<?xml version="1.0"?>
<books>
    <book>
        <author>Thomas Fleming
        </author>
        <title>Liberty! The American Revolution
        </title>
        <place of publication>New York; London
        </place of publication>
        <publisher>Viking
        </publisher>
        <date of publication>1997
        </date of publication>
        <ISBN>0-670-87021-8
        </ISBN>
        <pagination>394
        </pagination>
        <price="USA">$39.95
        </price>
    </book>
    <book>
    ...
    </book>
</books>
```

In this bibliographic description, one could leave out the ISBN, pagination, and price information to create a bibliography instead of a purchase request. One could include additional price elements, such as "Canadian dollar" or "British pound" or additional ISBNs for a paperback edition or an edition on acid-free paper. One could also add table of contents or other descriptive information or put the ISBN after the price. The ellipses toward the end of the description indicate that this is the first item in a purchase request and would be followed by one or more other books.

A user can create an element that will add all the individual price elements, when placing an order, to give a total estimated cost for the order. For example, using the xsl:value-of element (see Appendix 4) in an XSL template can compute generated text by extracting text from the source tree or by inserting the value of a string constant. The element computes the text by using a string expression that is specified as the value of the select attribute. For CSS2, one can enclose the string expression in curly braces ({ }) inside attribute values of literal result elements.

Database Loading and Reporting

Much of our structured information is stored in a database or spreadsheet. XML is a very good vehicle to deliver and exchange structured data because it is easily interpreted by a computer. Processing XML files can then allow people to generate a variety of reports or perform dynamic queries on data in text databases and generate output as needed, much as they can do with database managers.

While most programming languages can output text sequences relatively easily by enclosing those sequences in XML tags, features of the language and other issues can complicate reading an XML document. For example, the different ways a program uses white space (i. e. spaces, tabs, indentations, line breaks, carriage returns, columns, tables) to format a data file (as opposed to formatting the content of the document it contains) may cause problems of interpretation.

Developers of applications that accept XML as input should not have to write the code to interpret and parse the markup. Basically, parsing is just the interpretation of text. Most programming languages have the capability to incorporate software libraries; and a number of XML libraries already exist. An XML processor which is a processing module capable of interpreting XML data should be all that's needed to make the content of the document available to the application. The XML processor will also detect problems such as file formats the application cannot process or URLs that do not point to valid resources.

Event vs. Tree Processing

An application must interact with the XML processor to access parsed XML data. It must request specific information and may also instruct the XML processor to perform specific operations, such as changing the order of elements. An API enables this communication; but interfaces vary considerably in design. While each XML processor could include its own API design, this would result in a lot of overlap and redundancy. The development of a standard would eliminate an application's dependence on a particular XML processor and allow developers to transfer their skills.

As we'll see later, there are two different APIs being worked on for XML. They correspond to the two very different approaches to reading the content of an XML document. These are known as the "event-driven" and "tree-manipulation" techniques. The simplest way to process an XML document is the event-driven approach which processes the document in strict sequence. The XML processor reads the content as a stream of data and interprets the markup as it is encountered. When the processor encounters each element in the data stream, it evaluates it to determine what action to take or whether the application should perform some special action. Event-based processing is simple. It works fast; and it doesn't consume a lot of memory. However, its disadvantage is that it's impossible to look ahead to make decisions based on information that comes later in the data stream.

Unlike the event-driven approach, the tree approach processes the document as a whole. This approach to data structuring requires two passes through the data. The first pass parses the data and builds the data's internal tree structure. The second pass processes the data itself which allows an application to navigate the tree structure. This allows answering questions that require a look ahead in the data structure. For example, when a patron returns an overdue book, because the circulation clerk has access to the full document (the complete data tree), the clerk can easily determine if the patron has any other overdue items.

Out-of-sequence processing may be required to collect all the titles in a document for insertion at the start of the document as a table of contents. This would require a two-pass process where the titles are collected in the first pass and inserted where they are required in the second pass.

When the software has access to the entire XML document, in what may be termed a "random-access" method, it permits advanced processing options. The software that holds the document in memory organizes the content to make it easily searchable and manipulable. This allows querying the entire document and manipulating it in any order without multi-pass parsing. This produces instant access to any part of the document. XML-aware editors, pagination engines, and hypertext enabled browsers are some of the applications that benefit from this approach.

Because the tree structure approach stores the tree in memory, it is more powerful because it's easy to look ahead and get access to the whole document.

It can also be traversed in any way needed. However, the disadvantages of this approach are that it's more difficult to build a tree and then navigate it, it requires more memory, and it's slower because it requires two passes through the data. The W3C's standard tree-based API for XML and HTML is called the Document Object Model (DOM) which we'll discuss a little later.

Groves

A tree, or group of trees can be stored in a data structure called a grove. "Grove," which stands for "Graph Representation Of property ValuEs" mainly describes a series of trees (and other structures). Basically, a grove is an arbitrary subset of a document's element tree. Each node or branch represents an object of a specified type. Branches can be nested within one another as a package of information that conforms to a pre-defined template. The branches or nodes may be siblings of one another or completely unrelated except that they descend from the root element. For example, a node representing a person may contain the name, date of birth, and current address of that person. Each of these items is known as a property which has a name and a value and resembles an attribute.

If we compare the two processes to a motorist driving to a destination, event driven processing would be similar to the motorist reaching the destination by following road signs as he or she encounters them along the road. The tree-manipulation approach would be more like the driver studying a map before starting the journey to choose the best route in advance.

There are many pre-packaged software libraries that perform either of these types of manipulation that can be incorporated into applications. An API (Application Programming Interface) permits communication between the application and one of these libraries. Standards are being worked on for both event-driven and tree-driven methods, called SAX (Simple API for XML) and DOM (Document Object Model) respectively, to allow developers not to have to write different APIs every time they want to support newer and better products from different vendors.

Simple API for XML (SAX)

Consider a periodicals vendor, for example. To receive orders electronically or to process claims effectively and efficiently, the company must write programs to interface with the library systems of its customers. Each of these systems stores, processes, and outputs data in different ways; and the periodicals vendor's system must understand how this data is structured. Even using the MARC format, the variations in the use of the format (LC MARC, OCLC MARC, UK MARC, CANADIAN MARC, etc. and any local variations of implementation) can cause problems in the receipt and interpretation of that data.

XML could facilitate this data interchange through the use of a single API that would interpret the various data elements and process them correctly, regardless of the client library's system. Situations where the flow of data is essentially one way are ideal for a Simple API for XML. SAX is a standard interface for event-based XML parsing and the result of a collaborative effort by members of the XML-DEV mailing list, coordinated and finalized by David Megginson. It can be found at http://www.megginson.com/SAX/index.html or http://www.microstar.com/XML/SAX/spec.html

SAX implementations are currently available in Java and Python. The following parsers support SAX:

XML for Java (IBM)
XP (James Clark)
DXP (Datachannel)
AElfred (Microstar)
SXP (Silfide)
XML Library (Sun)
LotusXSL (IBM)

Thanks to third-party drivers, we can add two more parsers to the list:

Lark (Tim Bray)
MSXML (Microsoft)

Oracle Corp. announced a pair of parsers for C and C++ that will enable developers to access legacy information and transport it between applications using XML. These parsers complement existing ones for Java and Oracle's PL/SQL language. Oracle also announced tools that enable users to retrieve information from a database and publish it as XML.

SAX is not a parser per se. Rather, it sits on top of a parser. The API acts as a standard interface -- a sort of middle layer -- that mediates between some lower-level function(s) and some higher-level one(s). Although there's really nothing to demonstrate with SAX, it's a very important facility to have. For parsing XML, it allows a higher-level program to call any SAX-compliant parser and receive the parser's output in the same format, regardless of what the parser may be doing internally.

This is important because different parsers can and will often produce different results. This also applies to parsers based on identical specifications and built by developers of comparable talent and intelligence. This means that, if each parser produced its results in a different format, a higher-level program would require a differently-shaped "input pipe" for each one. SAX allows the parser to place its output in a standard sort of structure. This then lets a user choose any SAX-compliant parser to process the results in an application with a SAX "input pipe." The choice of SAX-compliant parser, then, will depend on which one will read the DTD and document without choking.

The XML processor contains a sub-unit called an entity manager. This entity manager locates those fragments of the document held in entity declarations or in other data files. It then replaces all references to them with the respective contents from the entity declarations or external data files. Some XML processors also include an integrity checker, or parser, which compares the content of the data file against the pre-defined document structure rules.

A common event-driven interface, such as SAX, can reduce the workload of the application developer and make it easy to replace one parser with another. More complex situations that produce exceptions or errors will require a much richer set of commands that operate in a more interactive fashion. For example, a purchase order that includes a vendor note field needs to be set aside for examination by a human before processing can continue.

Document Object Model (DOM)

XML employs a nested structure (tags properly nested inside other tags) that resembles very much the hierarchical data structures used in object-oriented programming. This makes XML and object-oriented programming compatible because they can store data sets within another data set. The Document Object Model (DOM), which builds on object-oriented programming principles, is a platform- and language-neutral interface that will allow programs and scripts to dynamically access and update the content, structure, and style of documents. The document can be further processed; and the results of that processing can be incorporated back into the presented page. DOM aims primarily to specify how future Web browsers and embedded scripts should access HTML and XML documents. DOM is being developed primarily to specify how web browsers and embedded scripts should access HTML and XML documents.

DOM consists of two parts. Document Object Model Level 1, which can be found at http://www.w3.org/TR/REC-DOM-Level-1/, and Document Object Model Level 2 (http://www.w3.org/TR/WD-DOM-Level-2/). Level 1 was accepted as a recommendation on October 1, 1998. Level 2 is still in the Working Draft stage.

Document Object Model Level 1 consists of two parts: Core and HTML. The Core DOM Level 1 section provides a low-level set of fundamental interfaces that can represent any structured document. It also defines extended interfaces for representing an XML document. All of the fundamental interfaces in the Core section must be implemented; but the extended XML interfaces need not be implemented by a DOM implementation that only provides access to HTML documents. A compliant DOM implementation that implements the extended XML interfaces is required to also implement the fundamental Core interfaces, but not the HTML interfaces.

The HTML Level 1 section provides additional, higher-level interfaces that are used with the fundamental interfaces defined in the Core Level 1 section to provide a more convenient view of an HTML document. A compliant implementation of the HTML DOM implements all of the fundamental Core interfaces as well as the HTML interfaces.

DOM Level 1 is concerned with defining an interface to document instance constructs common to both HTML and XML, including elements, attributes, comments, processing instructions, and text content. It lets authors add, delete, and change elements and their attributes as well as change the contents of elements. It only defines interfaces in a generic way, leaving the developers to implement the DOM spec for a given object oriented programming and scripting language, such as ECMAScript, VBScript, Java, C++, Perl, etc.

The DOM level 1 specification is currently limited to those methods that are needed for representing and manipulating structure and content. For example, going back to our example of a purchase request for a book, instead of adding a field for additional price elements, such as Canadian dollar or German mark, we could write a brief script that would use the DOM to convert U.S. prices to Canadian dollars or German marks. Other levels of the specification will need to address other pieces, such as the interfaces for internal and external subsets, the ability to validate, the ability to control rendering via style sheets, and the ability to control access.

The Document Object Model Level 2 builds on the Document Object Model Level 1. Level 2 is XML specific, adding interfaces for DTD markup (notation, element and attribute declarations, parameter entities, and conditional sections) and XML specific document markup (CDATA sections). The draft of the Document Object Model Level 2 does not have all of the interfaces that the final version will have. It contains interfaces for associating style sheets with a document, the Cascading Style Sheets object model, the Range object model, filters and iterators, and the Events object model.

Most tool vendors will likely implement the DOM API. They may use different languages (Java, VBSCript, etc.); but they will deal with the same objects, properties, and methods. Microsoft Internet Explorer 5 complies fully with the W3C DOM recommendation. Netscape also plans to support it in version 5. Vendors of editing tools and repositories (e.g. POET, Chrystal, Oracle, Texcel, etc.) will also support it. DataChannel, IBM, and Sun have already implemented the DOM API in their Java XML parsers.

The Document Object Model provides a standard set of objects for representing HTML and XML documents, a standard model of how these objects can be combined, and a standard interface for accessing and manipulating them. Vendors can support the DOM as an interface to their proprietary data structures and APIs; and content authors can write to the standard DOM interfaces rather than product-specific APIs, thus increasing interoperability on the Web.

Applications

XML can be used for almost any type of application, with new ones being developed continuously. Some typical applications include the following items. These examples are in no particular order of importance; but they include the most important or the most promising applications. Electronic commerce, which most experts consider the killer application for XML, will be covered separately in chapter 7.

Microsoft envisions using XML to distribute and update software. Customers can download software from the Internet, use it, and then discard it, resulting in what is called "zero install software."

When a Web browser downloads a Java applet or executes a piece of JavaScript code, in essence, it downloads a piece of software, uses it, and throws it away when someone closes the browser. Microsoft and Marimba expect to extend CSS to distribute software and binary code, such as audio, video, graphics, etc., via the Internet. Another application, called WebBroker, allows distributed software components to communicate with each other over the Internet.

Electronic Commerce Initiatives

To accompany the use of XML for electronic commerce applications, some companies are endorsing the Internet Open Trading Protocol (OTP). This protocol is an XML protocol for the exchange of financial transaction information, electronic payment, credit card information, and bank account details. Another candidate format and protocol for e-commerce is the Open Financial Exchange Specification (OFE).

General acceptance of electronic commerce initiatives depends to a large extent on the users' perceptions of security and privacy. The Platform for Privacy Preferences (P3P) offers a method for Web sites to use RDF (Resource Description Framework) and XML to identify the nature of their content (such as confidential or adult material). The Signed Document Markup Language (SDML), on the other hand, offers a means to electronically sign and verify electronic documents. This is similar to public key encryption mechanisms such as PGP (Pretty Good Privacy). A distinct document, XML-Signature Requirements, is still in working draft stage. This document lists the design principles, scope, and requirements for the XML Digital Signature specification. It includes requirements as they relate to the signature syntax, data model, format, cryptographic processing, and external requirements and coordination.

The mission of this working group is to develop an XML compliant syntax used for representing signatures on Web resources and portions of protocol messages (anything that can be referenced by a URI) and procedures for computing and verifying such signatures. Signatures will provide data integrity, authentication, and/or non-repudiability.

A Web publishing model called Push Media was once considered a breakthrough in Web publishing. A variation of that model, the Channel Definition Format (CDF), is expected to become a useful way of subscribing to Web sites that provide regularly updated information such as news, stock price quotations, etc.

The implementation of the Development Markup Language (DML) is expected to provide development organizations such as the WHO, UNESCO, the OECD, the Rockefeller Foundation and the World Bank a means to exchange information.

Multimedia and Heterogeneous Devices

There are also several applications targeting multimedia and heterogeneous devices. The Java Speech Markup Language (JSML) will permit adding structural information to synthesized speech to make it sound more natural. The Handheld Device Markup Language (HDML) would allow hand-held devices such as the PalmPilot, mobile telephones, and palm computers to browse the Web and communicate over the Internet as a sort of mini-HTML.

The XML Query Language (XML-QL) will implement SQL in XML. And Visual XML (VXML) will offer a way to describe Web sites and to publish them in the Virtual Reality Modeling Language (VRML) to produce a virtual 3D navigation experience on the browser.

An application called Open Tag will allow inserting XML tags in text to permit the extraction, translation, and re-insertion of translated material. The Translation Memory Exchange (TMX) provides a way to exchange vocabulary databases between software packages.

Specialized Applications

There are also several vertical applications already developed. The Chemical Markup Language (CML), which became the first XML dialect, represents and displays chemical molecule information, allowing chemists to manipulate and model atoms and molecules. It also supports the kinds of document elements found in scholarly papers, such as footnotes, citations, mathematical and chemical formulae, and glossary terms. The Bioinformatic Sequence Markup Language (BSML) represents and displays genetic sequence information. The Mathematics Markup Language (MathML) provides a markup language for mathematics that will make it easier and more user friendly than the TeX computer typesetting package which has dominated that market niche. There will also be a plethora of medical applications, such as Health Level 7 (HL7) which formats electronic patient records. This includes insurance information and treatment and billing data in addition to medical records.

Resource Description Framework

XML coupled with the Resource Description Framework (RDF) will provide better search engine capabilities. It will allow catalogers to describe the content and the content relationships available at a particular Web site, page, or digital library. Intelligent software agents will also be able to share and exchange information. It will also allow describing intellectual property rights of Web pages. It will help in describing collections of pages that represent a single logical "document" and facilitate rating content. It could also serve for expressing the privacy preferences of a user as well as the privacy policies of a Web site. RDF lays the foundation for processing metadata. It provides interoperability between applications that exchange machine-understandable information on the Web and emphasizes facilities to enable automated processing of Web resources.

The number of different XML applications is infinite. As no single browser can be expected to handle them all, we can expect that a core of the most popular DTDs will be supported. Specialized plug-in modules will handle other applications, particularly those for niche markets. Regular users will install these permanently. If these add-ons are written in Java, other users can upload them transparently as needed.

In this chapter, we considered some of the ways XML can manipulate data and possible reasons for doing so. We examined the two different approaches that an XML processor can follow and their corresponding APIs. We concluded with an overview of some XML applications. We now turn our attention to some of the issues related to managing XML documents before we explore XML's expected "killer app" – electronic commerce.

Chapter 6

Managing XML Documents

Many documents often undergo several file conversions and formats through the different stages of production. This is particularly true for published materials that get worked on by several editors, graphics designers, and layout specialists. These various stages are often expensive and time-consuming, particularly if the work has many complex formulas and charts. If the various parties could use the same electronic files, they could save a lot of time and cut production costs significantly.

On a broader level, anybody who has owned a computer for any length of time has had to deal with the issues of file conversion and incompatible formats when they upgrade equipment, purchase a new version of a favorite program, or change program altogether. These problems involve document management issues that XML can help resolve. XML includes features which software could use to simplify the creation and long-term management of documents. However, one should also keep in mind the general issues of document management that apply to all types of electronic documents, such as file naming conventions, grouping related documents in the same subdirectories, and so on.

This chapter will consider some of the document management issues related to the implementation of XML. It will look at different types of database architectures and discuss their utility for storing XML documents. It will examine the features of a document management system and an editorial system and discuss content management. It will then proceed to a discussion of managing resources on the network and making networked information more interoperable.

Document Management

The simplest way to manage XML documents is to store them in a fixed location within the file system. For example, all documents related to each other should be stored in the same directory. Images could be stored in a common image directory or grouped with the documents to which they relate. Media elements can be grouped together in a media directory or in separate directories by type of media. XML contains a URL based linking scheme that can facilitate file-to-file linking. A standard XML browser would be able to follow these links between documents.

Document management becomes a particularly important issue when XML is used to describe the content of large, complex documents that may be structured or semi-structured. These documents may have been authored by several people and created over a long period of time. They may have been destined for publication and eventual re-publication in a number of forms or in a variety of media. This type of information is most likely stored in electronic form and is too important to be misplaced, corrupted, or stolen. Therefore, it must be managed to protect it and to insure its future utility.

Controlling access to these types of documents is the simplest means to protect them; but it may sometimes be difficult or even impossible to control access to specific documents. It is certainly impossible to control access to parts of a document with currently available software. This is like saying that, in a library, a book is the smallest portion of information a patron can access, with no tables of contents or indexes. The short, cryptic file names required by older operating systems make it difficult to identify pertinent documents.

In environments where several people share access to the same files, two operators may access the same document simultaneously without their realizing it. Computer systems will generally retain only the changes made by the person who saves the work last. Existing systems generally don't store the status and history of a particular document. Retaining several versions of the same document usually becomes difficult to manage. When one operator finishes working on a document, there is often no means to notify a colleague that the document is ready for a subsequent step. Usually, co-workers develop work-arounds or procedures to alert each other to the status of a particular document.

In a networked environment, the management of entities can become a problem. Each entity has its own URL which identifies its fixed location. If the entity is moved to a new location, the URL must be edited to prevent dead links which have become the bane of Internet searchers. The use of a public identifier that assigns the entity a unique name could overcome this limitation. A catalog file that matches the name to a location address would then provide access.

Database Architecture

The addition of a simple database to a system could help solve some of these problems by storing metadata on the documents. This metadata could include the full document name, its current status, any keywords or other details that help identify the document, and a pointer to the file containing the document.

Such a database would be particularly useful to a front-end program that could use the content of the locator field to locate a file and pass it to another application to launch it. For example, a searcher could enter some keywords, receive a list of results, and select a particular title. The database search engine could then automatically transfer the entire document to a suitable editor for viewing or editing.

Flat-File or Relational Databases

A simple system might use a flat-file database which contains all the metadata in a single database table. However, a relational database would permit linking information across several database tables, making it easier to remove repeated and redundant information. For example, a single author probably created several documents. Storing the author's details with each document results in some redundancy, wasting storage space. Besides, relational databases tend to have more powerful query capabilities. Many use SQL (Structured Query Language) or even natural language search capabilities, making them easier to use.

A relational database used to store XML documents can break the documents into their hierarchical components for storage. The simplest way of storing this information uses a relational table which assigns a unique identifier to each record and a pseudo-element to each element. Other fields in the record contain a reference to its parent element and a child number that records its position in relation to its siblings. A more efficient and more complicated design would utilize multiple tables. The elements hierarchies, in this design, would usually be separate from the textual content. These tables would also store attribute values and other markup constructs.

However, relational databases have their limitations. First, it is not easy to represent hierarchically structured information in a tabular model. Storing the actual document inside the database tables has the advantage that the system protects the data to the same degree as the metadata, including it in incremental backups and hiding it from unauthorized users. But relational databases are not particularly well-suited to storing hierarchical data structures. XML elements have many relationships that do not correspond to a tabular representation. Each element has a parent and may have children which may have children of their own. Each element may also have siblings. Each element must also know its position in the hierarchy and its relationship to the other elements. While one could define fields to hold sequential and hierarchical relationships between elements, it would require a considerable amount of software support to deal with changes to a document. Many people think object databases are more appropriate for this kind of task because they do not require users to force data structures into a flat, tabular representation.

Object or Object-Relational Databases

Object database technology has emerged as an alternative to relational databases. Object databases use a much looser structure than the tables built from rows containing fields. They use uniquely identifiable units of information, called objects. These objects contain 'attributes' that each have a name and a value, just as in XML. Objects contain simple data or pointers to other objects.

Developed primarily for permanent storage of data objects created by object-oriented software applications, object database technology can also be used to store XML documents because it can describe sequential and hierarchical relationships more easily. As described previously, an XML document can be broken down into its constituent parts with attributes identifying the element name and an array of pointers identifying child elements in the order that they appear in the document.

The additional power of object database technology comes at the expense of performance. Many people consider this technology inadequate for "industrial strength" applications. Relational database vendors have risen to the challenge and developed the object-relational database. This approach uses an object layer that sits on top of a relational database. It compromises on both performance and object awareness. Most SGML/XML document management systems utilize object or object-relational database systems.

Document Management Systems

More advanced document management systems use relational databases which also keep track of different versions of documents and group projects. A document management system is like an enormous electronic filing cabinet that allows one to manage a whole mass of documents in a coherent manner. It not only stores the documents in a single repository with only a few keywords and a date for quick searching; it also keeps track of the documents' contents. It controls access to them by enforcing appropriate access rights for each user. It "checks-out" a requested document and locks it to prevent other users from accessing it and inadvertently overwriting any changes. It logs changes to a document when it is checked in after editing and allows users to locate key information quickly.

While one could easily manage a small hybrid XML/HTML Web site, it becomes more difficult to do so as the site grows, eventually becoming untenable at some point. As the site becomes larger, such as a company-wide intranet, it often becomes necessary to rely on software support such as a document management system for its maintenance. Document management systems that use SGML should be able to adapt easily to XML.

The full-text search capabilities of document management systems often consume enormous quantities of computing resources. XML would give document management systems a clearer picture of the contents of documents, allowing them to control larger sets of documents more efficiently. The ability to limit a search to individual elements would accelerate processing time to retrieve a document and reduce the number of false matches.

Search Engines

The most basic technique a search engine uses to locate documents that contain specified words or phrases is the inverted word index. An inverted word index is a simple list of all the words used in a document or collection of documents. The words are sorted alphabetically and have links to the documents containing them. The search engine usually records the exact location or locations of the terms in the original document.

An XML version of an inverted word index could also record the start and end location of each element embedded in the file. By comparing offset values, it could then determine which elements contain the specified terms and permit targeted searching. For example, one could locate all documents containing the word "Wellington" within an element called Name and "Waterloo" in the title.

FIND "Wellington" IN Name AND "Waterloo" IN Title

For the unsuspecting searcher, this would avoid all false matches to documents about footwear and military aircraft. Nor would an experienced searcher have to think about these possibilities or create a nested search strategy using the Boolean NOT operator.

Document Storage

XML makes it possible for document management systems to store documents as parts rather than as large chunks of often indecipherable information. An XML document management system should take account of both the physical (entities) and the logical (elements) organization of the documents. A document management tool written for XML could store documents as sets of elements within hierarchically organized databases. This provides the best opportunity to manage information resources effectively by avoiding redundancy of information.

Separating formatting information from the document's content makes it much easier and quicker for search engines and similar tools to parse the data without having to deal with formatting codes.

If the SGML world is any indicator, we can expect a wide range of XML document management systems will become available, offering a wide variety of approaches to document management. Informix, IBM, and Oracle produce database systems with object-relational tools that allow for the creation of a wide variety of data types. Some of these data types are rich enough to store XML documents as a set of small pieces that can be manipulated and that reflect the structure of the document, rather than as a chunk of text that requires a full parsing every time it is accessed.

XML/SGML-aware document management systems usually employ object or object-relational databases which allow users to access and edit part of a document in isolation. They also allow users to choose how large a unit to edit; and they permit two users to work on different parts of the same document at the same time. However, they do not let one user edit part of a document that another is already working on. A document management system may also be able to support some kind of versioning, keeping older documents with their older style sheet and giving newer documents a facelift.

A document management system doesn't care directly about style sheets; but it can keep track of which style sheet was used where because style sheets are just another link. A document management system that has access to style information makes it easy to foresee the impact of a significant change because it can warn designers which documents are about to receive the new style.

Even if a designer combines DTDs on a regular basis, one should create a separate style sheet for each DTD to prevent a user's machine from wasting time parsing style information it won't use. Developers can also save time in not searching through an enormous collection of styles. Selecting and implementing a naming convention and maintaining as much parallelism as possible between the DTDs and the style sheets will facilitate their management. This will make it easier to keep the DTDs and style sheets in separate directories and modify them or create a new DTD file and associated style sheet files. This can help prevent older documents from suddenly become invalid or the parts from disappearing.

Document management systems require humans to behave systematically. Making significant changes to a DTD could result in document files that the document system can't parse. One could write conversion programs; but that is no fun. Changing a significant library of documents by hand is even more tedious.

Editorial Systems

Some document management systems are designed for the 'factory' production of documents and incorporate, or link into, a system to track professional workflow. Many publishers use such a system, called an editorial system, for producing books, journals, and magazines. An editorial system would typically manage text files, images, and page layout files. It might also include features to track the amount of time an operator spends on each document.

An author or editor who wants to change or edit a single paragraph in a book should not need to check-out and open the entire book, or even one chapter. An editorial system that takes advantage of the structured nature of XML documents would make it possible to identify and access a single paragraph, to check-out the paragraph, and edit it separately from the rest of the chapter. This would let others access neighboring text blocks at the same time. A system that manages document components could 'pull apart' an XML document and store each part separately. This would allow a query to locate a specific part, such as a paragraph, and permit checking-out this single unit for editing. This feature would allow documents to share standard blocks of text, or to assemble documents from standard components. For example, equipment, such as engines, comes in almost limitless variations. The maintenance manuals for these items usually repeat the same blocks of text and could benefit from such a capability. Other environments that use a lot of repetitive boilerplate include legal and medical documents.

Content Management

The larger the collection of XML documents and the more varied the types of objects used, the more important management becomes. An emerging concept in the management and use of electronic files is that of content management. Content management consists of a set of processes and technologies that enable the creation and packaging of content, particularly for a dynamic and integrated environment like the Internet. Here, content could consist of a wide variety of information objects like documents, different types of media elements, applets, components, and so on.

Document management deals with maintaining and storing documents; and knowledge management is concerned with making information available through index, query, and search mechanisms. Content management shares some of the attributes of both document management (storing information) and knowledge management (accessing information); but it goes beyond them to create a system for re-using information for new and different purposes. The most common method of reusing content is through the cut-and-paste feature of word processors, browsers, and other applications. Other methods include linking and object linking and embedding (OLE).

Content management aims to facilitate the communication and information flow to all parties in an enterprise or even between organizations; so a content management system should allow content to be:

- created using familiar tools at any place within an organization
- structured and accessed in units appropriate to its meaning
- personalized
- reused as often and in any combination desired
- easily updated and kept current
- faithfully rendered in a variety of presentation media

The information content could be stored in a common repository where reusable units of information could be identified, assembled, formatted, and presented to the reader in a customized manner. Thus, reusable units could be reused as often and in as many different formats and combinations as necessary and can serve to generate new revenue. XML allows content management systems to personalize content presented to users. Each user could have his or her own style sheet or page template. By applying this style sheet or page template to an XML document, the reader can view selected content in a preferred format.

An XML page can define a service that links to other XML pages that define features. Each feature XML page can specify "behaviors,"such as how voice mail and e-mail relate to each other, for each of the services that offer that feature. The user can then pick the behaviors he or she likes and determine how a particular feature is requested or delivered simply by modifying an access-to-service page. Service providers, developers, and equipment vendors could also determine the behaviors that affect a single user.

External Entity Management

A networked environment often uses system identifiers to connect documents, resulting in possible problems if some of the documents are moved. It may be necessary to edit many local files to reflect the new locations if many documents refer to one or more files which get moved to another location. There are two techniques to deal with this problem. The first uses entities within entities. The second uses public identifiers in conjunction with an advanced entity manager module.

System Identifier Manipulation

Entities can replace fragments of a URL file path. One can define these entities in a single configuration file such as the following:

```
<!ENTITY charts "/xml/charts">
<!ENTITY images "/xml/fragments">
```

Then, when the documents are moved, only the configuration file needs to be edited. For example, one could include the list of declarations in each document instance by inserting both a declaration and a reference to it as in the following example (1):

```
<!DOCTYPE MyBook {
<!ENTITY % Library "config.xml">
%Library;
<!ENTITY XMLhistory SYSTEM "&fragments;/history.xml"
   NDATA TIFF>
<!ENTITY XMLhistoryChart SYSTEM "&charts;/history.tif"
   NDATA TIFF>
]>

<p> The history of XML is long and complex.</p>
&XMLhistory;
<p>This is illustrated in the following chart</p>
<image file="XMLhistoryChart">
```

One could also store the library file reference in a DTD to avoid editing each document instance if the library file itself gets moved.

Public Identifiers

Instead of using direct pointers to a file location, it is more elegant to employ an entity manager that uses public identifiers to locate external entities. The entries in catalog files make it easier to manage entities but they complicate the transfer of data over the Internet. We can illustrate the various means the entity manager can provide access to an external entity by using the example of an external DTD, as specified in the document type declaration. The following explanations apply equally to all external entity declarations.

A public identifier always requires a catalog file in which descriptive text replaces the file name in the document type declaration:

```
<!DOCTYPE mybook
    PUBLIC "-//MyCorp//DTD My Book//EN"
    "">
```

The keyword 'PUBLIC' identifies this example as a public identifier. The catalog file, then, matches the delimited text to a specific data file on the local system.

```
PUBLIC "-//MyCorp//DTD My Book//EN" C:\XML\MYBOOK.DTD
```

Catalog files make it easier to maintain XML document storage; but each XML-aware software application may use its own syntax for the catalog filing system. In this case, one must repeat the information for each application.

The SGML Open committee identified two problems related to locating entities on a system using catalog files. First, entity location details must be duplicated when each application that accesses SGML entities uses its own catalog format. Second, the application receiving an SGML document that consists of several files (not merged using SDIF) needs a simple method to identify the base document and all of its components.

The SGML Open group then produced a standard format to try to avoid this unnecessary duplication. The common catalog format described in the "SGML Open Technical Resolution 9401:1995 (Amendment 1 to TR9401)" solves both problems and allows many applications to share a single source of information. The format uses several identifier mappings that consist of a keyword, followed by a public identifier or entity name and an equivalent system identifier.

Formal Public Identifiers

The format of public identifiers (originally defined for use with SGML) has an optional formal definition. A formal public identifier has a rigid structure composed of several parts:

- the identifier type,
- the owner identifier,
- the public text class,
- the public text description, and
- the public text language.

If one is going to use a public identifier, it should conform strictly to the rules because adopting the look but not the rules of a formal public identifier would confuse people trying to interpret it.

The identifier type describes the status of the URL. A plus symbol, "+", in the identifier type field denotes a registered public identifier and guarantees that it is unique. (The ISO standard ISO 9070 describes how to register and generate a unique public identifier.) An ISO owner is identified by the text "ISO 8879:1986." If the identifier owner does not register, the identifier type contains the hyphen symbol, "-". A double solidus, "//", separates the identifier type from the rest of the name, as in the following examples:

<ENTITY .... PUBLIC "+//...">
<ENTITY .... PUBLIC "-//...">
<ENTITY .... PUBLIC "ISO 8879:1986//...">

The owner identifier gives the name of the person or organization that owns the content of the entity or just the identifier itself. ISO entities do not need to identify themselves in this field, as the identifier type has already established that ISO is the owner. Another double solidus separates the owner identifier from details following it:

"+//MyCorp//..."
"-//MyCorp//..."
"ISO 8879:1986//..."

The public text class consists of a keyword that specifies the type of information the entity contains. XML only uses four classes while SGML uses several others. These four public text classes are:

1. DTD which indicates that the remote data file contains a Document Type Definition that may also include declarations for elements, entities, and short references.

2. ENTITIES which indicates that the remote data file contains an entity set that, in turn, contains declarations only for entities. These entities are usually for character sets, such as the ISO sets.

3. NOTATION which indicates that the remote data file contains character data that documents the format of a notation.

4. TEXT which indicates that the remote data file contains a text entity. This entry consists of free text that provides additional information about the content of the external data.

The last component is the language which consists of a keyword from the list provided in ISO 639. The keyword for the English language, for example, is "EN". Again, a double solidus, "//", separates the language from the public text description. So, a complete public identifier might look something like this:

"-//MyCorp//ENTITIES Superscript Chars//EN"
......

Network Management

XML can also give Web pages some knowledge about the information they contain. By extending HTML to deliver semantic meaning to Web pages, rather than just formatted data, XML permits sophisticated searches that can distinguish multiple word meanings, such as the word "prince" to locate items about the musician, rather than Prince Edward Island, or a member of a royal family.

An important capability of XML is its potential to revolutionize distributed applications by providing a standard data-interchange format. Documents are generally meant to be human-readable, while application data is machine-readable. XML can deliver "smart data" to an application. If the XML documents are stored on a server, XML lets the client do more with it without returning to the server and tying up the network, as the same data can be loaded into various applications for different purposes.

Storing highly structured hierarchical data on a server in a hierarchical format is efficient because it doesn't have to be translated from other formats when needed. For example, structured data in a relational format has to be decomposed into component parts before delivery in the hierarchical format of XML. This means that a user can look at the same data in a spreadsheet for analysis, in accounting software for reporting, or in a Web page for viewing. Each application lets the user search, query, and manipulate the data with the client computer's own resources.

The Desktop Management Task Force (DMTF) put XML at the center of easier network management in October, 1998, when it released a specification that encodes its Common Information Model (CIM) schema in XML. CIM is the DMTF's standardized object-oriented information model aimed at letting users share management information among disparate platforms. It uses XML for encoding the data and HTTP for transporting the data. This will allow applications to retrieve CIM data using XML Web technology. Each compliant management tool will support XML and will therefore be able to exchange information easily in a common language understood by each participating platform, providing an unprecedented level of interoperability between management applications.

For example, Scriptics Corp.'s integration server uses XML to connect applications running on multiple platforms. Its BizConnect product includes a set of development tools, called BizConnect Author and an open-source scripting language called Tcl (pronounced "tickle"). BizConnect Author serves to write XML documents. Tcl attaches actions to XML elements. It is used to write business logic to establish workflow and to translate XML schemata between applications.

BizConnect tries to create a reusable software skeleton to support XML data exchanges by allowing companies to pass data directly from order entry systems to manufacturing resource-planning applications or other back-end systems through Web documents formatted in XML.

Most application servers do a poor job of connecting businesses or enterprises because they use proprietary protocols and data formats. That is why XML is important. By using XML as the data format and with standard Internet protocols, businesses can easily be integrated via the Internet. The next chapter will study in more detail how XML can help establish electronic commerce.

Notes

1. For further information, see: Bradley, Neil. *The XML Companion.* Harlow, England; Reading, MA: Addison-Wesley, c1998. p. 205-6.

Chapter 7

XML and Its Potential for E-Commerce

Electronic commerce has been touted as the killer application for XML; but it did not emerge with the development of the World Wide Web or the commercialization of the Internet. It has been around for over 25 years. It germinated in 1948 during the Berlin airlift when Ed Guilbert of the Department of Defense spearheaded the Transportation Data Coordinating Committee. This group needed to get the various modes of transportation (air, railroad, and ocean) to share data like schedules and to coordinate with each other and with their clients to effectively deliver goods and supplies. This eventually led to the establishment of the X12 committee which was accredited by ANSI (American National Standards Institute) in 1979. Large petroleum, banking, transportation, and retailing companies and the federal government soon began using X12 EDI (Electronic Data Interchange) to provide electronic forms and messages for shipping and purchasing. However, the book industry had already begun establishing communication standards in 1974.

It is easy to equate Electronic Data Interchange with electronic commerce; but EDI is really only one element of electronic commerce. We can describe Electronic Data Interchange as the communication of business information using "a collection of standard message formats and element dictionaries to exchange data." It is a set of standards that facilitate business-to-business processes such as ordering and fulfillment and financial transactions.

Electronic commerce, on the other hand, could be defined simply as "doing business electronically." The concept implies the exchange of information over computer networks; but it also involves online querying of supplier databases and the real-time integration of supply chains over the Internet and extranets. Electronic commerce, then, involves the buying and selling of products, information, and services over the Internet and extranets. It is part of the broader concept of e-business which encompasses the transformation of an organization's business and functional processes through the application of technologies, philosophies, and computing paradigms of the digital economy. E-business includes merchandise planning and analysis; order entry, tracking, and fulfillment; warehousing and inventory management; shipping, returns, and other logistics; pricing and promotions; financial accounting and reporting; customer service and customer relationship management; and knowledge management.

Electronic commerce could use structured communications (such as EDI) or unstructured messages (such as e-mail) to transmit information, data, databases, database access, or a combination of these. Electronic commerce comprises at least three types of communications: consumer to consumer, consumer to business, and business to business; and it implies electronic links between the various sources of information.

In this chapter, we shall begin by reviewing the origin and development of standards for Electronic Data Interchange, considering exceptions and variations that standards need to accommodate, and examining cost factors that affect implementation decisions. We shall then proceed to discuss conducting EDI over the Internet and the importance of metatags and data type definitions for interpreting data structures and improving functionality of business transactions. Then, we'll look at XML (eXtensible Markup Language) as a proposal to broaden the applicability of transacting business over the Internet by bringing EDI to the desktop. We shall consider how XML could work for EDI over the Internet and the benefits that it could effect. We shall conclude with a brief look at some of the efforts to use XML to effect electronic commerce.

Origin and Development of EDI Standards

Although humans have long envisioned that computers would improve communication and data interchange for commercial applications, reality usually required developing custom interfaces for each different system to facilitate transactions with suppliers and customers. In the six years from its creation, in 1974, until the Book Industry Systems Advisory Committee (BISAC) became a committee of the Book Industry Study Group (BISG) in June, 1980, BISAC aimed to streamline the ordering and supply of books and printed materials. It developed formats for purchase orders, order acknowledgment, invoice, title status, payment advice, frontlist diskette, data transmission protocols, royalty statement, and sales reporting.

In 1979, the American National Standards Institute (ANSI) Accredited Standards Committee (ASC) X12 began to develop uniform standards for the electronic exchange of business transactions in standards known as electronic data interchange (EDI). Around 1983, the major BISAC members wanted BISAC to develop formats based on the X12 formats to allow the book industry to follow standards comparable to other industries and supported by standardized "translators" and value added networks.

The ASC X12 committee meets three times a year to develop and maintain EDI standards. The committee's main objective is to "develop standards to facilitate electronic interchange relating to such business transactions as order placement and processing, shipping and receiving information, invoicing, and payment and cash application data, and data to and from entities involved in general business, finance, insurance, education, and state and federal governments."

The ASC X12 standards aim to facilitate electronic commercial transactions by establishing a common, uniform business language for computers to communicate. They comprise more than 300 transaction sets that allow businesses to execute nearly every type of business-to-business operation electronically, such as orders, invoices, customs declarations, statistics, insurance documents, bills of transport, and many health care transactions. They are often the electronic equivalent of the preprinted forms sold in stationery stores. The goal was not to replace paper forms with electronic equivalents but to allow businesses the flexibility to re-engineer how work is processed in order to gain efficiencies of working electronically via EDI. Those companies that closely examined their work processes benefitted more than those who just replaced paper forms with electronic forms.

The EDI standards have even become recognized internationally and have received endorsement by the United Nations which developed the UN/EDIFACT standard (United Nations Standard Messages Directory for Electronic Data Interchange for Administration, Commerce, and Transportation), in many respects, based on lessons learned in X12's development experiences. UN/EDIFACT messages use predefined field identifiers which must occur in a predefined sequence. Some users claim it is less robust than ANSI ASC X12. Others say the opposite; but its widespread acceptance makes it viable. EDI got further endorsement in 1997, when President Clinton decreed that all U.S. government procurement be accomplished via electronic commerce. The U.S. government then began moving toward adopting and implementing X12 and UN/EDIFACT.

Exceptions and Variations

Every industry has its own way of doing things. Not only must international standards accommodate possible variations by industry and company, they must also take into consideration each country's own set of exceptions. Even within the same industry, many companies operate differently. It is not uncommon to add comments on a purchase order to clarify what one wants or the terms of delivery, for example. Standard EDI messages must support these comments and many other options that make them very complex. This complexity resulting from the differences between trading partners and the related costs of programming or mapping data discourage many companies from implementing EDI.

Also, in the development of international EDI standards, language becomes important. We take it for granted that the data elements and syntax use English. English is a dominant language in the business world and the Internet is based on English syntax and almost every program is coded in English language friendly computer languages. However, have French or Chinese vendors and buyers, for example, been willing to use English? Should the data elements be language-neutral or should multiple naming conventions and syntaxes be used?

Cost Factors

EDI messages serve to exchange documents or data between companies. However, different organization store their data in different formats and representations (data layouts). One company may store its data in a relational database, for example, and may have to map it differently for transmission via EDI. Such mapping can be very involved and costly.

In addition to the costs of programming and data mapping, companies incur high costs in acquiring and implementing EDI. These costs include hardware, setup, EDI-enabling software, transaction service fees, telecommunications charges, and annual software maintenance contracts that the ongoing evolution of EDI standards require.

Companies must realize sizable savings to break even. Because the quantity of documents exchanged determines the amount of savings, large companies that process many transactions can offset their costs in a relatively short time. Small and medium-sized organizations, on the other hand, will find it harder to justify EDI. Large companies can offset the cost of EDI through increased efficiency. Smaller companies, however, can find the costs prohibitive, excluding them from revenue opportunities. For example, some large companies, particularly those in low-margin retail businesses such as Wal-Mart and Kmart, refuse to conduct business with any company that does not use EDI.

The wide range of interfaces employed by users further complicates implementation and support. In addition to creating, or contracting with a software vendor to create a custom interface for every trading partner with which it exchanges data, a company must deal with the complexity and expense of custom user interfaces that must be created for each new form, document, or process. This makes EDI a complicated and expensive proposition for many.

EDI Over the Internet

EDI has been most successful in vertical markets and in business-to-business transactions with a large number of interactions. The advent of the Internet and its use for business applications changed how people interact when they exchange goods and services. EDI is no longer restricted to business-to-business communications. The Internet has introduced many new ways of trading, allowing interaction between groups that previously could not afford to trade with one another economically. The same principles apply to all commercial transactions, whether the consumer is an end-user, a manufacturer, a service organization, a governmental agency, or a virtual organization. So all participants in the electronic marketplace should be able to transact business with the same ease.

The Internet Engineering Task Force (IETF), a large open international community of network designers, operators, vendors, and researchers concerned with the evolution of the Internet architecture and the smooth operation of the Internet, is part of The Internet Society that develops Internet standards. Much of its work is done in its working groups. Some of these groups are concerned with business communications and should be making recommendations for implementing standards of commerce over the Internet.

A major challenge to performing EDI on the Internet is to reduce the cost of doing EDI enough to allow small and medium-sized organizations to realize savings also. The goal is to enable them to perform EDI transactions with only a browser and an Internet connection. The application of XML to EDI on the Internet promises to do just that.

Metatags and Data Type Definitions

By using metatags, such as those employed in XML, to identify data elements, companies can tag their data once and use it with any number of applications, such as in the preparation of catalogs, purchase orders, and invoices. The tags also allow for distinguishing different meanings for the same word. For example, one could use different tags to identify the term "pocketbook" as a purse, a billfold or wallet, or a small book. The term “date” with no qualifiers could indicate an order date, a shipping date, a received date, a social engagement or a person’s companion on such an outing, or even a fruit.

XML tags and attributes can incorporate long-established messaging structures and rules that vary from industry to industry into Web-based documents for Electronic Data Interchange between trading partners. This could streamline the purchase of goods and open the supply chain to any trading partner with an Internet connection and an XML-capable browser. It could also facilitate the entry of smaller companies into the electronic marketplace by allowing vendors to offer products directly to a buyer, effectively removing the middleman because all processing is done on the client side, the buyer's computer. Buyers and suppliers of all sizes can participate in commerce over the Internet because it does not require the use of proprietary technologies.

As the ANSI ASC X12 and UN/EDIFACT standards have already devised structured messages for most types of business transactions, it's very likely that they can serve as the basis for XML Data Type Definitions for commercial transactions. The DTD and metatags will be most useful when used by a number of people and tools. However, in the real world, people often agree to comply with the standards, then modify them a little or a lot to suit their own needs and those with whom they're communicating. While XML offers a high degree of flexibility, industry users will need to resolve how to establish data dictionaries and how to make those dictionaries usable to general-purpose electronic commerce applications. A data dictionary defines every data element and helps map data from one application to another.

X12 and UN/EDIFACT both offer a data dictionary that meets general business requirements, The data mapping between these dictionaries is well-defined, resulting in their becoming two of the most widely used standards for transmitting EDI data. Brian Green, Secretary of the European Book Sector EDI Group, expects that EDItEUR will soon begin developing neutral data dictionaries which will allow UN/EDIFACT tags to be used by XML or any other language that uses metatags for book industry transactions over the Internet. XML could facilitate mapping to neutral data dictionaries and allow small-to-medium sized companies to take advantage of EDI at a much lower cost and commitment of resources.

Part of the problem of implementing EDI in the library market is the very complex product description. As we saw in chapter one, the MARC format could easily serve as the DTD for library applications as it contains all the information needed by librarians and anybody working in the book trade (see Appendix 4). However, any changes will likely occur over a long period of time; and business requirements will determine how this will all evolve.

A DTD could serve to specify the structure of a document and how to interpret it, much like a template. The creation of a template in this fashion could enable users to create the equivalent of EDI messages without the labor and cost of extensive data mapping. Libraries process an enormous number of transactions; but the relatively low price per item and small margins currently militate against widespread implementation of EDI. By implementing XML, however, librarians and vendors can process messages on the client side, further reducing costs and processing overhead.

Metatags Mean Greater Functionality

Today's search engines can easily extract information from textual databases and Web pages. But some form of tagging system must be used to retrieve "fielded" data accurately. XML/EDI and the use of metatags permit using structured data along with unstructured text in the same document. These metatags allow searching, decoding, manipulating, and displaying data consistently and correctly without the need to create special interfaces. They could also enhance commerce on the Web by adding new dimensions not currently available. For example, if online booksellers use a standard set of metatags to mark titles, descriptions, and prices, buyers could quickly search all of the online bookstores for the lowest price on a book with a single command.

Books and music have emerged as the leading goods and services sold on the Internet. Zona Research Inc. (Redwood City, CA) estimated that book sales over the Internet totaled $181 million for the fourth quarter of 1997, with music trailing at $47 million (1). It forecasts that the number of businesses planning to conduct business over the Internet will grow by 34%. International Data Corp. (Framingham, MA) estimates that the amount of commerce conducted over the Internet will increase from $2.6 billion in 1996 to $220 billion in 2001 (2). The market is so lucrative that Barnes & Noble is reportedly prepared to lose $7 million dollars a year to build market share online (3). Robert Krulwich, in an ABC News broadcast on November 24, 1998, reported that Barnes & Noble's customer base stood at 930,000 compared to Amazon's 4,500,000. While Amazon's new customers increased by 1,200,000 in the previous few months, Barnes & Noble only added 210,000. However, this was before the purchase of half of Barnesandnoble.com by Bertelsmann.

Online catalogs are the first applications taking advantage of XML; and major European wholesalers publish monthly multimedia CD-ROM stock catalogs. Most of these catalogs allow users to build order files and to transmit them in EDI formats, normally using direct dial-up. But the number of consumers who purchase goods over the Internet account for only one percent of the consumer market.

Today, only sites that have been specifically set up to exchange information can conduct EDI transactions. XML would permit exchanging data regardless of the computing systems or accounting applications being used. The intent of XML/EDI is to establish a standard for unambiguous commercial electronic data interchange that is open and accessible to all and which can satisfy the full breadth of business needs. Marty Tenenbaum, chairman of CommerceNet, says that "it's essential that all these systems talk to each other; and they can't today, except at the level of HTML."

Planning for the Future

Attaining these objectives requires using a scalable or extensible means that will satisfy current needs as well as future requirements, including the ability to incorporate new technologies and business needs as they emerge. The selected technology also needs to be widely and freely available to ensure widespread adoption. XML has been proposed as a solution that meets these requirements.

The W3C published a specification for a formal Document Object Model (DOM) for XML documents in October, 1997, as we saw in chapter five. This model provides a standardized API (application programming interface) for XML-based tools. It indicates that XML-coded electronic forms may become the main method of capturing and coding EDI information.

Using XML for Electronic Data Interchange

The use of XML for the interchange of commercial EDI messages follows several stages. First, one must identify the suitable data sets to use in electronic business transactions, such as the ones in the UN/EDIFACT standards. Then, one develops the XML data type definitions (DTDs) that specify how the fields that are to form a particular class of EDI messages relate to one another. Third, come the definitions of the relationships of the fields and of application-specific extensions to standard message types. Then, one creates the specific types of electronic business messages, validates the contents of messages, and transmits and receives electronic business messages. Finally, one could use DataBots, data manipulation agents, to process electronic business messages.

Because XML/EDI is a standard for formatting documents, it leaves the method for how to store or transmit these documents to the underlying applications. One can use FTP, Email (SMTP), HTTP, or another method to transmit XML/EDI transactions just as any other document. One can transmit them via a value added network (VAN), Intranet (WAN), or Internet. One could also store them on diskette or another transportable medium for shipment via courier or the mail.

XML could use the XML protocol as its "data interchange modeling" layer and the XSL protocol as its "presentation" layer. XML would allow the data to interface with EDI; but the underlying processing would remain EDI. XML could function with traditional methods of EDI and could support all standard Internet transport mechanisms such as IP routing, HTTP, FTP, and SMTP. It uses programming tools such as Java and ActiveX to permit data sharing between programs; and it uses agent technologies to manipulate, parse, map, and search for data.

Benefits

Leading the list of benefits of using XML for e-commerce is that it allows people and companies to exchange information more clearly and completely than was possible with previous formats. XML lets heterogeneous systems communicate with each other through a common language which describes the templates and associated conversion rules. This means that users can conduct business transactions at the client level on desktop computers with a general-purpose document or web browser as the user interface. Even though XML/EDI allows distributed processing capabilities, it also supports centralized functions. It lets users be more independent, permitting them to define and issue documents rather than relying on data processing specialists to do so.

Instead of having to create templates and interfaces for each trading partner, traditional EDI service providers just need to interface their products to XML/EDI templates. As companies implement XML/EDI to provide simpler-to-use types of transaction tools, businesses that fail to incorporate XML/EDI into their operations will limit their growth and may see their products eliminated from the marketplace because their competition will have made it easier to do business with them.

Because XML/EDI supports legacy or traditional EDI systems by definition, companies that use UN/EDIFACT or ASC X12 standards can continue to use their systems. XML is more verbose than X12; but it's not as position-dependent. The tags for each value identify the data element each value represents, thereby reducing dependence on CGI scripts and screen-specific programming and eliminating any problems of lost data. Users can create a conversion routine (gateway) between the subsystems that use UN/EDIFACT or ASC X12 and those that use XML/EDI to interface with clients or suppliers who are reluctant to adopt XML/EDI. Business requirements will determine how this will all evolve; and the conversion will likely occur over a long period of time.

Most EDI systems have tended to use fixed-length or delimited field database structures for ease of processing. Business partners used to mail tapes to each other regularly. Data transmission has improved dramatically; and companies now connect over data networks. However, the form of the information hasn't changed much. XML gives businesses more flexibility than their current systems can offer. It also gives them an opportunity to create simple standards that can be extended to cover additional data structures as necessary.

Efforts to Use XML for Electronic Commerce

XML is just text that can provide content and structure for most types of information. The basic difference between XML and HTML is that XML defines the content rather than the presentation. Some people say that using XML to encode data is like using ASCII. The format is so flexible that almost any organization can develop its own "standard;" but implementing several versions of XML within the same industry, without some sort of coordination, makes it difficult to share data and results in incompatible applications. EDI and bar code standards have laid a solid foundation for electronic transactions for many industries; and XML could allow industries to complement these efforts with industry-specific electronic business interfaces.

These interfaces would encompass basic transactional data as well as all aspects of commercial relationships. Each industry needs to develop a set of business standards to allow the electronic systems of the participants to interface and work together to achieve greater cost efficiencies. The problems in describing information using XML range from deciding what to describe to deciding what to name each field. After users agree on how to implement these matters, they need to tag their data so another party or application can recognize the data transmitted.

The W3C XML recommendation uses the term "tags" to describe the markup; but the more precise terms would be "elements" and "attributes." The specification describes how to create the markup tags and outlines the benefits of using them to describe data. It leaves it to individual developers and industries to determine names for the tags, what they describe, and how other developers must format information for processing. XML calls these special descriptions schemas which can be considered industry-specific DTDs.

Schemas

Schemas are used to share intentions about what is expected and how information received for a particular event will be validated. They are designed to make it easier to share data between databases and between databases and other applications by allowing authors to be more specific in describing the types of data in the documents. For example, while a DTD identifies the variables in a document such as a number, a schema further specifies the data and valid ranges, such as the type of number (floating, fixed, or date). The schema working document consists of two parts: XML Schema Part 1: Structures and XML Schema Part 2: Datatypes. The Schema: Structures group is focusing on how to combine individual data elements into entities while the Schema: Datatype group is focusing on how the individual data elements are defined. Schema: Datatype will make it possible to create user-defined data types.

While it may seem exciting to create one's own DTD to perform certain functions, a developer should always check the availability of an industry standard DTD. A proprietary DTD can offer a customized solution to particular systems and needs; but it may also cut one off from the rest of the industry. XML markup is most useful when many people and tools use the same DTD.

"Commerce applications have the most at stake in standardization because search engines and other applications must be able to count on the same elements having the same meaning no matter what the source. Compatibility will be more important than a perfect solution in most cases involving multiple organizations. (5)"

The trend seems to be toward more, rather than fewer, XML extension standards. Dozens of industry organizations and standards bodies are actively engaged in defining XML schemas for application integration. These groups include electronic commerce consortia such as the Organization for the Advancement of Structured Information Standards (OASIS), RosettaNet, CommerceNet (commercenet.com), CommerceXML (cXML.org), and the OBI (Open Buying on the Internet) Consortium, as well as software industry groups like the Open Applications Group Inc. (OAG) (manufacturing industry) and Object Management Group Inc. (OMG); vertical industry standards bodies like EDItEUR (book industry), ACORD (Agency-Company Organization for Research and Development) (insurance), and HL7 (health care); and individual software companies like Ariba Inc., Microsoft Corp., and Commerce One Inc. Each one of these organizations wants to define a standard set of XML documents used in an interchange between applications or between companies. They also want to position themselves as hubs for e-commerce by hosting repositories of XML schemas that businesses will use, expecting that the hand that writes the schema rules the world.

Any effort to get these different standards bodies to adopt a consistent set of semantics across their existing set of XML schemas will be difficult. For example, to get the OAG, ACORD, and Commerce One to adopt a consistent use of an address element across their respective XML schemas would require two committee votes and a modification to a shipping software application. Past industry efforts to get different standards bodies to consolidate around a consistent set of business objects were unsuccessful for these reasons. We shall now consider some of the more prominent efforts to implement XML as a means to reduce procurement costs when buying goods over the Internet.

E-Commerce Consortia

xml.org

The Organization for the Advancement of Structured Information Standards (OASIS) is a non-profit international standards consortium founded in 1993 and based in Boston, MA. It introduced xml.org on May 25, 1998 with the intent "to advance the open interchange of documents and structured information objects." The xml.org Web site aims to reduce fragmentation by establishing an open, distributed system for enabling the use of XML in electronic commerce and other industrial applications and by serving as a central clearinghouse on the

Web to coordinate XML news and proposals for tags. It is designed to provide a credible source of accurate, timely information about the application of XML in industrial and commercial settings and to serve as a reference repository for XML specifications such as vocabularies, DTDs, schemas, and namespaces.

Members of the xml.org Steering Committee, which held its first meeting on July 13, 1999, include Commerce One, DataChannel, Documentum, Graphic Communications Association, IBM, Oracle, SAP AG, SoftQuad, and Sun Microsystems. The OASIS Registry and Repository Technical Committee seeks to specify a registry for some sets of XML-related entities, including, but not limited to, DTDs and schemas with appropriate interfaces that enable searching on the contents of a repository of those entities. The registry and repository will cooperate and interoperate with other registries and repositories that comply with this specification.

xml.org's most important function is to serve as a trusted, secure, persistent repository and registry for DTDs, namespaces, schemas, and other specifications that must be accessible globally to enable the use of XML for data exchange within particular industries. The site intends to encourage the use of XML for electronic commerce by providing a key piece of the necessary infrastructure and then to serve as a model for an extensible, distributed system of registry/repository sites based on the same architecture, thereby avoiding the duplication of effort in developing tag sets for particular industries.

RosettaNet

Another initiative, RosettaNet, was launched in February of 1998 to develop and deploy open and common business process interfaces. RosettaNet (http://www.rosettanet.org) is an independent, self-funded, non-profit consortium dedicated to the development and deployment of standard electronic commerce interfaces to allow supply chain partners to exchange data.

RosettaNet focuses on building a master dictionary to define properties for products, partners, and business transactions, particularly for the computer parts industry and the IT supply chain. This master dictionary together with the exchange protocols that implement the framework serve to support the electronic communication between business partners, a process that RosettaNet calls Partner Interface Process or PIP. RosettaNet's Partner Interface Process consists of four stages:

1. Business Process Modeling

   Business Process Modeling involves identifying and quantifying the individual elements of a business process. One creates a clearly defined model of the supply chain partner interfaces as they exist today, a process called "as is" modeling. This model reflects the results of extensive research at every level of the supply chain. It is then analyzed to identify any misalignments or inefficiencies.

2. Business Process Analysis

A "generic to-be" process emerges from the analysis of the detailed "as is" model. This new model shows the opportunities for re-alignment in the form of a Partner Interface Process (PIP) target list. It also estimates the business impact of implementing the resulting PIPs (savings as a function of time and money).

3. PIP Development

The purpose of each PIP is to provide common business/data models and documents that enable system developers to implement RosettaNet eBusiness interfaces. Each PIP includes:

- a) XML document(s) based on Implementation Framework DTDs, specifying PIP service(s), transactions(s) , and messages(s) which include dictionary properties;
- b) Class and sequence diagrams in UML;
- c) Validation tool; and
- d) Implementation guide.

4. Dictionaries

Two data dictionaries are being developed to provide a common set of properties required by PIPs. The first is a technical properties dictionary (technical specifications for all product categories). The second is a business properties dictionary which includes catalog properties, partner properties (attributes used to describe supply chain partner companies), and business transaction properties. These dictionaries, coupled with the RosettaNet Implementation Framework (exchange protocol), form the basis for each RosettaNet Partner Interface Process (PIPs).

As with the other efforts discussed here, RosettaNet has a Managing Board consisting of twenty-eight individuals representing global members of the IT supply chain. They include hardware manufacturers, software publishers, distributors, resellers, system integrators, end-users, technology providers, financial institutions, and shippers. The RosettaNet Managing Board is responsible for defining the interface development projects and setting the initiative's priorities. They are also primarily responsible for promoting and implementing these interfaces in their own companies and with their eBusiness partners.

Commerce XML

Commerce XML (cXML), a collaboration between buyers, suppliers, and Internet technology companies, has the backing of more than 40 Web vendors, including Sterling Commerce, Vignette, Ariba, Web Methods, InterWorld, Ironside, Extricity, Poet Software, and Saqqara Systems; some of Ariba's suppliers such as Chevron Corp., Cisco, and Bristol-Myers Squibb Co.; and Ariba customers such as 1Nine Systems, Anderson Unicom Group, barnesandnoble.com, BT Office Products International, CAP, a division of the McGraw-Hill Construction Information Group, Chemdex Corporation, Collabria, Compucom, ComputerLiteracy.com, Cort Furniture Rental, Harbinger Corporation, Life Technologies, NCR Systemedia Group, Office Depot, RoweCom, Staples, and US Technologies.

cXML is a set of XML DTDs that allow businesses to exchange common business documents in a standard form. It describes the characteristics of items available for sale and enables the development of 'intelligent shopping agents.' It intends to reduce online business trading costs by streamlining the process of digitally exchanging catalog content and transactions in a secure manner. Because it supports all supplier content and catalog models, cXML allows suppliers to provide customers with selective access to personalized catalog content while maintaining their unique branding and competitive differentiation.

cXML also defines twelve common business processes for the exchange of transaction information. These processes include purchase orders, change orders, order acknowledgments, status updates, ship notifications, invoices, and payment transactions. cXML has a lower-cost of implementation than EDI because it uses XML to leverage a company's existing HTML e-commerce infrastructure and software to allow buyers to access supplier Web sites from within a buy-side application, for example. This functionality lets buyers see their contracted items, private prices, and access libraries of products or tools to specify product configurations. XML's neutrality permits easy conversion to other formats, such as EDI, if needed. Some people like to think of cXML as 'bar coding' for the Web but with a greater variety of tools to identify and describe products.

OBI Consortium

OBI is a standard meant to facilitate business-to-business Internet commerce for high-volume, low cost goods and services, such as office and lab supplies, computer equipment, temporary help, and other indirect materials not involved in the production process. It allows a buyer to place orders with a seller without having to make any proprietary adjustments to the respective software systems.

The OBI Consortium has 62 members to manage the standard. They include Ford Motor Co., Johnson & Johnson, Lockheed Martin Corp., and MasterCard International, Inc. as well as various software vendors such as Dell Computer Corp., IBM, Microsoft Corp., and Netscape Communications Corp.

Vertical Industries

EDItEUR, the European Book Sector EDI Group, will soon begin developing data neutral data dictionaries which will allow UN/EDIFACT tags to be used by XML or any other language that uses metatags for transactions in the book industry. The Book Industry Study Advisory Committee (BISAC), a committee of the Book Industry Study Group, Inc., may assist in this effort, although it has not yet made any formal commitments.

ASC X12 and CommerceNet produced a White Paper in August, 1998, that suggested that XML should be applied to the X12 EDI standards. However, when they tried to do so, the ASC X12 representatives found semantic problems with the current EDI standards that precluded the development of unique XML tags. For example, in X12, "Title" could refer to the title of a book or of its author. Recently announced XML/EDI applications include: Edifecs Commerce's Guideline XML (gXML) for EDIFACT and X12; and a Danish Consortium's XCAT Project which includes an Internet demo of the use of XML to convert an EDIFACT message.

Book Data Limited, faced with more queries and updates to its database than it could handle conveniently, decided to take a fresh approach by using XML-based systems. They wanted technology that allowed visitors to access their Book Place database from different URLs and to be able to see different Web sites without knowing they were looking at the Book Place database. Book Place is an online interface to a database of every UK book in print. So visitors could search Book Place and have the impression they are searching the Penguin bookshop, for example. They could also get customized catalogs or insert links and URLs into their documents or databases that pull data from the Book Place database, capitalizing on a common source to publish many products with little additional effort. For example, one could search the database, sort by sales volume, and rank the number of sales per book to identify best sellers. This could be done on an hourly basis, resulting in HTML pages that are constantly changing. One could also input a series of ISBNs and let the system select five at random, but always a different five, to present the title, jacket, and a link into the database. The jackets can be made to spin around while the page is static or every time a user visits the page.

ACORD (Agency-Company Organization for Research and Development) is responsible for developing and promoting forms, EDI standards, and data standards for the insurance industry. Its standards define much of the data needed to produce personal and commercial lines transactions including policy, claims, and underwriting.

Individual Software Companies

BizTalk.org

Microsoft Corp., the dominant software supplier, had the same idea as OASIS and unveiled BizTalk.org one day before the introduction of xml.org. Microsoft intends BizTalk.org to serve as the main repository for its own XML tags and products as well as those of its partners in e-business, such as Ariba and Commerce One.

BizTalk provides the dialects and dictionaries to make sense of a document's content. It also serves as a framework for consistent XML schemas, and as a means for registering such schemas for wide use. It consists of three major elements: the framework description, a repository for BizTalk schemas, and requirements for submitting schemas to automated validation bots.

BizTalk Framework: BizTalk uses an XML framework, called the Microsoft® BizTalk™ Framework, to integrate applications and for electronic commerce. BizTalk Framework consists of a technical specification that defines a way to use XML in a consistent way, a code set that defines a small number of mandatory and optional XML tags used in messages sent between applications that all BizTalk XML documents must contain in order to take advantage of the framework, and the www.biztalk.org web portal.

BizTalk Framework defines a way of thinking about and managing the information flows that move between business processes, like the flow between the procurement process in one business and the order fulfillment process in another. Since business processes are supported by software applications, this information flow equates directly to making two or more applications work together. The technical term for this is application integration.

BizTalk Framework aims to create industry-standard definitions for business processes such as corporate purchasing, product catalogs and promotional campaigns. Each XML document must contain a root tag that identifies the document as complying with the BizTalk specifications. Like any XML document, but unlike HTML documents, all opening tags must have a corresponding closing tag.

The special XML tags, or codes, defined by the BizTalk Framework address issues that are common to all integration solutions. The BizTalk Framework schema syntax includes optional guidelines for message handling tags used for BizTalk Processes. BizTalk Framework can also inherit XML elements from other BizTalk schemas for schema aggregation and customization. The specifications add e-commerce-specific tags for protocol-level information necessary for business messages, tools, and industry-specific documents.

Microsoft Corp., other software companies, and industry standards bodies will be expected to use the BizTalk Framework to produce XML schemas in a consistent manner. BizTalk Framework schemas are business documents and messages expressed in XML. They will be registered and stored on the BizTalk.org Web site; and BizTalk will act sort of like a brand name. The BizTalk Framework itself is not a standard here. XML is the standard. BizTalk Framework's goal is simply to accelerate the rapid adoption of XML.

BizTalk Repository: The BizTalk Repository will let developers submit schemas to an automated validation process, which posts it as either a public or a private schema. Anyone can then go to the site and search for public schemas by author, company, product industry, process, and document type.

By formalizing the process of expressing business process interchanges in a consistent and extensible format, the BizTalk Framework makes it easier for independent software vendors and developers to map from one business process to another. This enables a wide variety of industries that use open standards, such as XML, to implement electronic interchange — the exchange of XML documents and messages between trading partners or applications — more quickly and easily.

Until applications have native support for XML, these types of BizTalk Framework interchanges will require layered software that transforms native data types into XML and then performs the XML document routing. Microsoft anticipates that the vast majority of interchanges implemented using the BizTalk Framework will use a simple HTTP post transport. However, businesses can also use other transports including FTP and message queuing technologies, including IBM Corp.'s MQSeries and the Microsoft Message Queue Server.

This data exchange requires the development and adoption of industry-specific schemas; but the important point is that BizTalk Framework interchanges do not require any specific software product from any individual software vendor. BizTalk will enable communications between Microsoft products (including a new BizTalk server), third-party products, internal enterprise systems, and Web portals and Web sites from Microsoft and others.

BizTalk is backed by Barnes & Noble Inc., Best Buy Co. Inc., Claris Corp., Commerce One Inc., Concur Technologies Inc., Dell Computer Corp., DataChannel Inc., Eddie Bauer Inc., Emercis Corp., Harbinger Corp., J.D. Edwards & Co., Level 8 Systems, PeopleSoft, Sharp Electronics Corp., SAP, Sterling Commerce, Vitria Technology Inc., Web Methods, and other vendors and customers. SAP AG will work with Microsoft to create common XML semantics to get SAP's Business Framework and Business Applications Programming Interface to communicate with Microsoft's Component Object Model and BizTalk.

XML is such a key technology that it will be a native part of Microsoft's products. BizTalk will find its way into nearly all Microsoft products and Web sites, including a new BizTalk server (part of Microsoft's Back Office product line) that is set to ship shortly after Windows 2000. But BizTalk will not be a Windows-specific technology.

Microsoft's supporters see BizTalk as an altruistic attempt to jump-start XML; but its opponents see it as another attempt at world domination. They say that Microsoft intends to establish a version of XML that can only be accessed through The Microsoft Network. They also claim that any XML schemas defined through BizTalk will become Microsoft's intellectual property.

BizTalk Steering Committee: A supervisory group, called the BizTalk Steering Committee, oversees BizTalk.org to prevent anyone from subverting either the BizTalk Framework or XML in proprietary ways to benefit one vendor or group of customers more than another. The Steering Committee consists of a selected group of standards bodies, government agencies, software vendors, and select corporate customers. The members were chosen for their experience, insight, interest, and commitment to the BizTalk Framework. They review proposed changes to specifications prior to their posting on the BizTalk.org site.

Authors should know that if they write an XML application based on BizTalk or any other schema, they may have to re-write the application – or part of it – to conform to the W3C specification. This may be done through the use of a template which would convert data from one vendor's version of XML Schema to another. Microsoft plans to provide a migration path to the W3C's XML Schema when it gets finalized.

Other Efforts

Commerce One has a product, BuySite, that automates the procurement process from requisition to order. Its MarketSite software then automates the interaction with the supplier from order placement to payment. The company expects that integrating XML will reduce operational costs and increase efficiency because of its ability to define products so buyers can search online catalogs to identify the right product at the right price.

DataChannel is working with IBM, Commerce One, and General Motors Corp. to develop two pilot programs that use XML to send bid requests and buy non-critical supplies. General Motors will be able to tap data from legacy, relational, and enterprise resource planning databases. It will then be able to use the Automotive Network Exchange to exchange documents with its 100,000 suppliers.

Vignette Corp., of Austin, TX, proposed Information and Content Exchange (ICE) as an XML-based protocol to govern business-to-business e-commerce transactions. ICE allows defining the data elements for the terms of sale and the methodology for passing copies of an offer between the negotiating parties until the terms of sale are finally agreed upon. For example, a subscription agent might propose the delivery schedule and related nonfinancial terms of a subscription as an offer encapsulated within an XML document. The agent could offer to download the content of a given subscription each weeknight from 2 A.M. to 3 A.M. A subscriber might gather content from other sources at that time and make a counteroffer to download the content one hour later.

Supporters include Vignette Corp., Adobe Systems Inc., Channelware Inc., Sun Microsystems Inc., Microsoft Corp., National Semiconductor Corp., CNET Inc., Hollinger International Inc., News Internet Services, Preview Travel Inc., Tribune Media Services, and ZDNet.

Since ICE is a transport protocol and not a set of DTDs, it would complement, rather than compete with, cXML, BizTalk, and Common Business Libraries (CBL). Commerce One bought XML vendor Veo Systems Inc. which introduced CBL. CommerceNet's eCo group's uses CBL as part of its eCo Framework specification for business-to-business commerce. CommerceOne is Ariba's main competitor. Ariba, as we have seen, supports cXML; but it has completed the integration of cXML with the Microsoft BizTalk Framework to deliver a complete schema for conducting business-to-business transactions.

Sequoia Software's Interchange 2000 includes three modules: iAcquire, iManage, and iPresent. iAcquire is a set of data acquisition, capture, and transformation tools. iManage provides a core data repository, indexing, security, and workflow and data distribution tools. iPresent offers methods for publishing information individually or as part of an aggregated report. The three modules make extensive use of XML schemas and data objects.

Microsoft's Internet Explorer 5.0 already supports XML, XSL, DTDs, and XML schemas. Netscape Navigator/Mozilla 5.x will do so when it is released. Netscape also plans to add XML support to its CommerceXpert line of Internet commerce applications.

Mobile Devices

Not to be outdone by these efforts, wireless equipment makers are working on a variant of XML, called WXML or WML, that aims to increase the speed of

Internet communications. WXML aims to allow Web sites coded with WXML to recognize the memory, modem, and display limitations of the user's phone or other handheld device. It will then transmit text synopses instead of pages laden with graphics. It lets developers create content once that can run on any device instead of having to rely on packaged content designed for specific devices. Cell-phone companies Motorola, Lucent Technologies, and AT&T have created another variant called VXML that will convert XML text into speech. This will allow car phone users to keep their eyes on the road and still access Internet services with wireless devices.

Bluestone Software's free XML parser (www.palm.com or www.metrowerks.com) will allow Palm computers to process XML documents. Its Visual XML tools will allow creating XML documents as drag-and-drop operations instead of Java coding and allow developers to tie XML files to SAP or mainframe databases. Integration of XML on handheld devices gives users greater flexibility in exchanging information with corporate servers. A query entered on a Palm III could be converted to XML and sent to a database for searching. The database could respond with an XML document which could then be converted back and displayed on the PalmPilot.

eXtensible Forms Description Language

In another development, Unisoft Wares, a specialist in electronic forms, presented an initial specification draft of the eXtensible Forms Description Language (XFDL) to the W3C in September, 1998. XFDL describes how to represent digitally the complex documents used in business and government to allow computers to exchange data. XFDL supports precise layouts, supporting documentation, error checking, digital signatures, and an audit trail for transactions.

The most important difference between HTML forms and XForms is XForms' "computability" that allows performing calculations on numerical data entered in designated fields. XForms also adds scripting capabilities to HTML, potentially making all elements dynamic because a script may change the content and attribute values of elements. XForm hidden fields can be structured XML which can have arbitrary attributes and child nodes of their own. But XForms can also eliminate the need for special hidden fields because any element can effectively act as a hidden field. One can write a style sheet to use the value of an element while not displaying the element. XForms can also allow any element to trigger form submission instead of a Submit button or the less common image map in HTML. That is because any linking element can be extended to be a form element.

JetForm Corp. announced a competing specification to add forms processing to XML. Its XML Forms Architecture (XFA) acts as a bridge between the XML data structure and presentation formats. XFA is backed by security vendors Entrust, PenOp, Silanis, and VeriSign.

While work is being done to develop schemas and define how business-to-business and consumer transactions will operate in XML, there are a number of ancillary issues that need resolution before e-commerce becomes widely accepted and implemented. Security issues, not only of the systems and communications media, but also the verification and authentication of individuals are major obstacles to overcoming consumer skepticism. Developments in network security, personal identification and authentication, encryption, and the digital exchange of funds exceed the scope of this book (6). However, we should note that the W3C approved the Digital Signature (DSig) recommendation on August 20, 1999.

Digital Signature

DSig details a standard format for supporting digitally signed, machine-readable transactions. Signatures provide data integrity, authentication, and/or non-repudiability. DSig focuses on signature syntax, data model, format, cryptographic processing, and external requirements and coordination. It is based on earlier technology, called Platform for Internet Content Selection (PICS), that was initially used to filter objectionable Web sites. PICS started by labeling site content. DSig, on the other hand, assures recipients that the sender stands behind the information in the document. The American Bar Association has also developed Digital Signature Guidelines for transaction record security. These guidelines deal with authorization, document authentication, and signer authentication.

Vendors such as Microsoft and Ariba would like to control XML e-commerce standards; but IT managers who want to automate purchasing don't seem to care which standard wins as long as one emerges. While it may be difficult to get any industry to implement a common set of semantics and dictionaries across different XML schemas, it might be possible for each industry to agree on two or three competing schemas. They could also publish maps that would convert between competing schemas.

While business partners will find it an easy decision to adopt XML and common schemas to trade data with one another, competitive companies, like online bookstores, auction sites, computer stores, etc., may drag their feet before exposing data in a standard way. Eventually, consumer demand will require that companies provide data in a standard way so they can search for and compare prices across multiple sites. Companies unwilling to accede to these demands will lose business.

It is important to note that, in all of these efforts, many of the same names keep recurring. The major players are hedging their bets and support several initiatives, trying to be "on the winning side" in defining the standards. This allows them to be on the cutting edge and to have an advantage over competitors when the standards are finalized. The players are all sizeable companies that stand to profit greatly from early entry into the XML e-commerce market. They expect that the early entrants will tend to dominate the market. Librarians are conspicuously absent from these deliberations. This is partly due to the high costs of membership in these standards organizations plus the costs of time and travel to attend meetings. These costs contrast sharply with the little gain librarians expect to receive. Instead, librarians expect their systems vendors and suppliers to participate in – or at least keep informed of -- the trends and developments in these areas so they can obtain compliant systems at an opportune time.

In this chapter, we briefly reviewed the history of the development of standards for Electronic Data Interchange, considered some of the exceptions and variations that standards need to account for, and examined cost factors that affect decisions to implement EDI. We discussed how the Internet is changing expectations for electronic business transactions; and we considered XML as an emerging solution. By applying object-oriented technology to EDI, XML uses metatags and data type definitions to interpret data structures and improve the functionality of business transactions. XML promises to allow clients to implement EDI with a minimum of effort, thereby reducing costs; but implementation will not occur overnight. The change will be gradual and evolutionary rather than revolutionary. As applications get updated and modified with XML code, these solutions will eventually replace older, more cumbersome applications. In the meantime, several companies and organizations have begun to adapt existing standards or to prepare DTDs for use with XML. We have looked at the efforts of several consortia, vertical industries, and individual software companies. We also mentioned related efforts to extend XML and e-commerce applications to mobile devices and for applications that use many forms. Many companies are also working on getting XML ready for mainstream computer users.

Notes

1. *LAN Times Online* 1/98.

2. Hurley, Hanna. EDI Takes to the Internet. *Network Magazine*. October 1998. p. 36.

3. *The Search for Digital Excellence* / James P. Ware et al. New York: McGraw-Hill, 1998. p. 29.

4. Messmer, Ellen. Software Aims to Bridge EDI/XML Traffic. *Network World.* July 13, 1998. p. 6.

5. St. Laurent, Simon. *XML: A Primer*. Foster City, CA: MIS Press, 1998. p. 177.

6. For an overview of the issues of personal verification and authentication, encryption, secure electronic telecommunications, and "digital money" see Desmarais, Norman. Body Language, Security, and E-Commerce. *Library Hi Tech.* [In press.]

Chapter 8

Getting Started

Anybody who can tag for HTML can tag for XML. The names of the tags differ; but the principles remain the same. There are some differences, though, as pointed out in the various chapters of this book. One main difference is that XML requires that all tags have proper ending tags. Another is XML's case sensitivity. Some people say that XML is like HTML on steroids because of the increased functionality it provides. Yet, it is relatively simple to use. Authors can code XML with a simple ASCII editor in the same way they do for HTML.

Tagging XML documents by hand can be a long, tedious task for anybody working with more than a few documents. Most users will want to speed the process and avoid having to tag everything manually. Most word processors will eventually support XML as a native import/export format, if not their default format. This will let authors save documents in XML, just as they can do for HTML, without having to learn to use a new tool. However, the coding may be terrible; and the results may not display as expected, as is often the case with HTML created with a word processor. WordPerfect 9, part of Corel's Office 2000 suite, will let users create, validate, and save SGML and XML documents. Its WYSIWYG environment will offer a separate window to view a structured-tree view with an easy-to-read layout of the full document. Its editing environment will also include wizards and automatic element insertion.

A word processor like WordPerfect 9 may be adequate for authors who only need to create or modify XML documents occasionally. Those who need to create robust XML documents for Web pages and publications will need a hardier product that has more powerful document creation, editing, importing, and exporting features. Those who are familiar with authoring documents for the Web may want to rely on a familiar Web authoring tool, as most, if not all, of these tools will support XML. For example, Microstar's Near & Far Designer (http://www.microstar.com) offers such a graphical tool that evolved from the SGML world to support XML. In fact, some of the products discussed below incorporate Near & Far Designer.

In this chapter, we concentrate on the different types of tools available specifically to create XML documents. We shall look at four classes of tools: content development programs, application development packages, databases, and schema development kits. The first two may seem to overlap quite a bit and have many of the same features. We could draw parallels with other types of programs that have general release versions and professional versions. Content development tools are designed to create XML content and other tools. Application development tools are designed to build XML-based applications. The previous chapter covered efforts to promote the development of schemas for particular industries and their storage in repositories for general accessibility. Readers should also refer there for more information about schemas, their importance, and efforts to promote their development and adoption.

This chapter aims to outline the most important classes of development tools and the questions to consider when selecting a tool for a particular purpose. It does not present an exhaustive list, as it seems that new tools become available almost daily. The most commonly used class of tools will probably be those that could be considered XML word processors that will serve to create and edit XML documents.

Content Development

XMetaL

The most promising tool for creating XML documents is SoftQuad's XMetaL (http://www.softquad.com). XMetaL extends authoring technology to XML in much the same way its HoTMetaL product extended it to HTML. It is different from a Web authoring tool; it is a production tool for creating XML and SGML content. XMetaL allows users with little or no knowledge of XML to create content or data as easily as they would use a word processor. This is a critical step if XML is to become a common data format. XMetaL is the closest product to an XML word processor currently on the market. While it may not always produce perfect results, the outcome is very good; and the product takes a great step in making XML usable by a broad audience.

XMetaL follows the same general idea as XML: to create content that an XML conversion engine could distribute in a variety of formats, including HTML or as a database record. Because the content is already in proper XML syntax, XMetaL ensures error-free conversion by the central engine.

XMetaL's basic word processing interface has four important tools. First, it includes a fully functioning style sheet editor that supports the W3C CSS2 specification. It contains a macro tool that lets authors use Document Object Model (DOM) and Component Object Model (COM) controls. This helps to integrate XML documents with databases and document management systems. Finally, a Customization editor lets authors customize keyboard strokes. This is useful both for creating specific DTDs and for general productivity.

XMetaL includes all the basic word processing tools, such as cut and paste, search and replace, auto-save, and multilevel undo. The spell check feature only checks the written text, not the XML syntax codes, resulting in fewer words to examine and correct. The style sheet editor handles basic visual presentation tasks for XML documents that will be distributed via a browser. It is geared mostly toward text display, as most XML presentation tools; but it can produce visually pleasing displays. Authors can insert a style sheet link into a document to have the browser then refer to that style sheet for visual processing.

XMetaL provides an easy entry into XML. It lets authors write documents in "normal" mode, hiding the XML syntax or displaying it as desired. An author can view documents in a browser preview mode, but only using Internet Explorer 5. SoftQuad plans to make XMetaL browser independent when more browsers can support XML.

SoftQuad distinguishes itself from its competitors in two important areas: price and ease of use. XMetaL's price is about the same as many office suites. Its user interface looks like a WYSIWYG word processing package, minimizing the learning curve and allowing authors to work in native XML or SGML environments with pretty much the same level of comfort as using a word processor.

Competitors

XMetaL's competitors include Arbortext (AdeptEditor), Interleaf (BladeRunner), Stilo Technology (WebWriter), Adobe (FrameMaker+SGML), Vervet Logic (XML Pro), and Datalogic (FrameLink). Most of these offerings are oriented more to larger enterprises and commercial developers. Arbortext Inc.'s AdeptEditor offers an integrated suite that lets authors write in MS-Word or other common authoring tools and then import the results into AdeptEditor. An SGML editor with XML editing capabilities, it has a lot of additional SGML editing features and is more complicated than other products.

RightDoc's RightDoc (http://www.rightdoc.com) product is a business document writer that uses XML and CSS as its file formats. It can integrate more intelligent data into documents using ODBC and output to HTML, PDF, and PostScript formats.

IPNet Solutions (http://www.ipnetsolutions.com) uses XML in its IPNet Suite electronic commerce products. These products support DTDs, XML data import and export, and automatic XML to HTML translation as well as translation between XML and other business formats.

Microsoft's FrontPage 2000 Web authoring tool (http://www.microsoft.com/frontpage/trial) should also support XML as will Adobe Systems's Adobe GoLive (http://www.adobe.com) and Macromedia's Fireworks 2 Web graphics production tool (http://www.macromedia.com).

Webb Interactive Services (http://www.webb.net) intends to make XML publishing on the Web painless for small businesses and advertisers. Its CommunityWare/XML Publisher takes a template-based approach which uses XML and XSL to create up to five design alternatives in real time. The program automatically converts XML to HTML for today's browsers. Webb expects that building an XML repository will lay the foundation for value-added services, such as comparison shopping and dynamic shopping guides.

BladeRunner

Interleaf's BladeRunner (http://www.informix.com), co-developed with Microstar Software, also offers a WYSIWYG authoring environment and publishing engine for XML. It uses XML as its technology backbone and Microsoft Word for content creation, permitting users without any XML expertise to create new XML DTDs via a graphical tree representation, and valid XML documents by generating a document template. Authors can create documents in popular word processor formats, Interleaf 6, FrameMaker, Lotus Notes, and other formats and import them into BladeRunner. An author can use Microsoft Word as an XML editor to create a Word template that matches the XML DTD. The author can then create structured information without having to know XML and save the Word file as an XML document. Before check-in to the Content Repository, the document undergoes a final validation.

BladeRunner ensures that the document complies with a specified DTD by prompting the author through the creation of the proper elements. It can convert existing SGML documents with their DTDs into valid XML DTDs. It can import and export validated XML documents as well as output in various electronic and printed forms, including HTML, XML, and PDF. BladeRunner runs on Windows NT and includes Near & Far Designer, Microstar's DTD design tool, as one of its components.

BladeRunner's Content Management Module deals in "Managed Units" of information which it stores in hierarchies (chapters, parts, etc.). It supports a range of object- and relational databases, supports version control, and combines an XSL style sheet with XML content. It allows searching in many ways and manages links and references to different information units. A set of workflow tools allows designing and tracking editorial content. Editors and reviewers can define, allocate, and schedule tasks using a graphical user interface; and they can browse assignments remotely through standard Web browsers. An assembly engine facilitates the assembly, creation, and styling of XML documents which are then transformed to the appropriate media.

The BladeRunner Content Publishing Module combines an XSL style sheet with XML content for display. It includes a set of menu-driven Styler&Composer tools to create and link XSL style sheets with XML content and to preview the document layout. The Composer's drag-and-drop feature makes it easy to make changes and to reorder elements.

The Web DataBlade module lets users store and query XML structures in their native hierarchical format instead of in flat relational tables. Informix is developing an XML metadata repository and a server-based workflow engine that will permit embedding rules in XML documents.

Stilo Technology, Ltd.'s WebWriter is another XML editor that offers the ability to build an XML document and accompanying DTD; but it isn't as polished as XMetaL. XMetaL is the easiest XML editor to use and can only get better with subsequent versions.

XML Pro

While XMetaL can be used by the average computer user, XML Pro, as its name indicates, is aimed at experienced developers. Vervet Logic (http://www.vervet.com) produced one of the first XML editors commercially available and has built upon its pioneering efforts. XML Pro is a more sophisticated product with a clean visual development environment. Its interface consists of three main views: the document window, the attribute view, and the edit window. The document window resides beneath the familiar toolbar and menu lists. It consists of two views: a hierarchical view, on the left, that shows the entire document structure and an attribute view, on the right, that shows all the information about a highlighted element. These change dynamically depending on the data point selected. The edit window appears beneath the attribute view. This is where authors add text content to the document.

XML Pro offers data manipulation features similar to those in XMetaL; but its interface isn't nearly as friendly. It supports drag and drop, undo, and cutting and pasting; but all these functions are aimed more at developers rather than writers.

XML Pro seems to assume that one creates data somewhere else and that XML Pro enters the picture with the XML conversion process.

XMetaL and AdeptEditor both focus on the document in a workspace similar to that of a word processor. XML Pro focuses on the data, emphasizing the XML structure hierarchy. While one can view DTDs in XML Pro, one cannot edit them. Other products have built-in DTD editors; but XML Pro omits this feature. It offers this feature as a bundle with Microstar's Near & Far Designer, a tool designed specifically for DTD editing.

In addition to viewing DTDs, XML Pro also parses them. This ensures that any imported DTDs comply with XML rules for validity; but XML Pro won't open a DTD if it encounters a problem. However, unlike the approach taken by some other XML editing tools, XML Pro will open XML files with errors and immediately provide an error pointer marking the problem.

XML Pro includes IBM's XML4J parser which means that XML Pro will be able to comply easily with the W3C's DOM and SAX interfaces. It also supports IBM's Java Development Kit which is a requirement since XML Pro is written in Java. This makes XML Pro easier to develop advanced XML/Java applications. It also allows the product to run on Windows, Solaris, and Linux. XML Pro stands out in its ability to combine Java and XML.

XML Pro is a full-featured XML editing package that seems aimed at application development rather than content development. Both schools depend on the XML specification; but one product cannot serve both purposes. As an application development program, XML Pro has such basic features that it's almost a beginner's package. Developers accustomed to the Windows environment may find that it lacks bells and whistles they have come to expect of their development products.

This is not a product for XML novices or HTML developers accustomed to WYSIWYG tools. XML Pro requires that developers have a clear understanding of both XML's basic building blocks and the DTDs associated with edited documents.

XML Spy

Icon Information-Systems's XML Spy offers a better product than XML Pro at a fraction of the cost. XML Spy is available only as a Web download (http://www.xmlspy.com) and is quickly gaining the attention in the shareware community.

XML Spy's workspace, much like XML Pro's, consists of three windows. The Grid View, similar to XML Pro's tree view, shows all the elements in a document in a hierarchical tree view. It allows editing any elements represented here. The Source view displays the document in its XML source form. It lets users customize color highlighting of syntax elements, making it easy to change a document quickly. The Browser view lets an author view a document still under construction using Internet Explorer 5. This view fully supports CSS, XSL, Extensible HTML (XHTML), and XML namespaces, making it a very nice feature. It can even display the various views inside the XML Spy workspace without toggling back and forth to Internet Explorer 5.

XML Spy's menus and toolbars offer the usual assortment of find/replace, cut and paste, and print editing tools. It also has the ability to save an XML document with invalid syntax or other problems. This might seem trivial; but it's a very nice feature because it lets an XML developer save a document at the end of a work session instead of having to resolve every problem before saving the work.

Besides being an XML document editor, XML Spy can also create and edit DTDs without an extra-cost bundling option as XML Pro. It also lets an author edit a DTD at the same time as the XML document that uses it, providing a great cause-effect view. XML Spy even allows simultaneous editing of multiple XML documents.

XML Spy only runs on the Windows platform which makes it able to use RichEdit 3.0 in Windows 2000 for both faster display updates and foreign writing system support. It also uses Microsoft's MSXML Parser to edit and validate DTDs. While this is still a fairly standards-neutral solution, Microsoft's track record with open Web standards can raise concerns about MSXML as a long-term standard. XML Spy lacks robust creation tools like a database editing tool and publishing wizard, and support for CSS, XHTML, or a Java editor. However, Icon intends XML Spy to serve as a validation tool rather than a content creation tool; and XML Spy excels as a validation tool.

Application Development

Visual XML

Bluestone Software Inc.'s Visual-XML (http://www.bluestone.com) is a powerful application development tool. Content development tools like XMetaL are designed to create XML content and other tools. Application development tools, like Visual XML, are designed to build XML-based applications. In this respect, Visual XML stands out as an application development tool just as XMetaL excels as a content development tool.

Visual XML includes several sample XML applications to illustrate just what an XML application should be. These applications are basically DTDs designed for specific functions, such as a purchase order DTD that interfaces with a back-end database, rather than just document types. The samples also serve in the Help and Tutorial feature to introduce programmers to the nuances of both XML and its development environment.

Visual XML's easily navigable graphical interface contains all the tools an author could possibly need to manipulate XML data and to combine it with outside data sources. It includes step-by-step development wizards and built-in editors that make it easier to build XML applications. These tools also improve productivity through faster prototyping and deployment of XML-based communications. The Database Publishing wizard, for example, helps users build XML documents from database sources.

The wizards and editors perform full editing functions on raw XML code, DTD specifications, SQL queries, and even Java. They also integrate well with other utilities in Bluestone's products, such as its Sapphire/Web application server platform, its XML-Server platform, and its XwingML development tool, designed to merge Java and XML code. The Process wizard, for example, lets users configure one-time or automatic publishing of XML documents and data into an XML server, such as Bluestone's XML-Server. Visual XML is definitely optimized to take advantage of it.

Somebody wanting to capitalize on XML's benefits for the workplace or for supply-chain automation might also consider the Bluestone server environment. This server consists of the XML integration server and Sapphire/Web for large-scale distributed applications. Bluestone even places hooks to this product in its documentation, pointing to its XML-Server's Universal Listener Framework (ULF) which represents the communications portion of the document conversion engine.

ULF lets a developer create Java and XML applications that generate, receive, and act upon communications, such as purchase or fulfillment orders. This could permit companies of any size to improve their Internet-commerce effectiveness. It allows importing XML data from a variety of sources into the Server and ULF and using any communications protocol, including HTTP, Secure Sockets Layer, Java Messaging Service, IBM's MQSeries messaging product, and e-mail to field requests and trigger responses that will automate the supply chain or office workflow. It even includes a scheduler so users can manage batch processing of XML documents along multiple destination lines.

Visual XML can facilitate mapping between documents based on different DTDs; but Bluestone only uses IBM's XML Translation Generator. Because of licensing restrictions, it does not come with the product; but buyers can download it from the alphaWorks Web site (alphaWorks.ibm.com). Bluestone intends to strengthen the transformation engines and capabilities in future releases.

A database object browser enhances the SQL editor to provide a full view of back-end database tables and columns, as well as data objects and static queries or stored procedures. While Visual XML is not adequate for database administration, its tools suffice to optimize an XML application for use with any SQL-compliant database. Bluestone's Visual XML offers an excellent tool for XML developers looking for a professional-level application development environment.

XML Authority

People who want to build DTDs for various industries face a dilemma. Many developers now consider DTDs unwieldy and want to exploit XML for more than just text documents. The W3C is working on draft specifications of XML schemas which could eventually make DTDs obsolete and negate any work already done on DTDs. However, moving directly to schema creation could also prove futile if the standard doesn't catch on. Extensibility Inc. (http://www.extensibility.com) aims to solve this dilemma with its XML Authority which supports both DTDs and all major emerging schema formats.

XML Authority is the first tool that is effectively standards-blind when it comes to DTDs. It considers traditional DTDs and each of the new schemas [XML-Data, the data definition markup language (DDML), document content definitions (DCDs), and schemas for object-oriented XML (SOX)] as essentially the same thing from a development point of view. It takes advantage of the wide base of commonality among these standards and minimizes each standard's syntax and feature idiosyncrasies.

XML Authority's workspace isn't as elegant as Bluestone's; but it's still open, fairly customizable, and targeted to XML developers rather than content editors. It consists of two basic windows. The top window lets the developer view the entire DTD or schema in a hierarchical tree structure. The second window, on the bottom, divides the work into columns for easier editing. When the work is complete, a developer can save it either as a typical DTD or in any other format.

XML Authority can also open and modify any existing schemas or DTDs and then save them in either native or converted format; but it still requires the user to be familiar with each DTD or schema's individual syntax and feature quirks. While the product includes a common set of tools to manipulate DTDs and schemas, it may require the developer to use them on his or her own once DTDs begin to diverge into their own peculiarities. Each schema will have an underlying foundation of XML syntax; but each one will be geared toward different purposes. The most frequently encountered one, aside from traditional

DTDs, will most likely be XML-Data. That is because Microsoft's Internet Explorer 5 supports a subset of XML-Data which has support for data-typing and namespaces as well as XML syntax.

XML Authority offers a great common viewing and basic editing package for DTDs and schemas; but tools like Visual XML and even XML Spy have more features and are better suited for in-depth DTD and XML application design work.

IBM

IBM made a series of development tools available for free on its alphaWorks Web site (http://www.alphaWorks.ibm.com/Home). These tools all focus on Java. While XML aims to make data portable, Java aims to make programs portable. The tools include:

- The Bean Markup Language (BML), an XML-based language for creating, accessing, and configuring JavaBeans. It includes an interpreter that reads the script to create the Bean hierarchy and a compiler to create the Java code.

- The XML Editor Maker which automatically builds a visual Java editor which then serves to edit XML documents based on a user's customized DTD.

- DataCraft, an application development/database tool that lets information stored in databases, like Microsoft Access, be viewed and published in XML.

- Dynamic XML with Java which enables developers to put Java code within their XML documents. It adds dynamic behavior to XML for server-side Java and Java-based workflow applications.

- PatML which matches and replaces patterns for transforming large XML documents to smaller XML subsets or other document types. The user can specify the rules for the patterns and transformations.

- TeXML which provides mapping from XML into the TeX formatting language which is used primarily in academia for page layout and printing.

- XML Bean Maker which enables developers to generate a JavaBean and all of its necessary Java classes for a given DTD.

- XML TreeDiff which lets users organize XML programming hierarchies and find differences between Document Object Model trees quickly.

- The XML Productivity Kit for Java works with IBM's XML Parser for Java to build XML applications using Java.

Databases

Text processing represents a large portion of electronic publishing; but it is not the only vehicle. Databases also comprise a large and important source of electronic information. Several software companies are concentrating on developing XML products for database content, particularly for the business sector.

Database vendors Oracle and IBM support XML natively and application servers, such as Object Design's eXcelon, offer XML capabilities for application integration, data interchange, and e-commerce. Two ODBMS vendors in particular -- Object Design and POET Software -- have moved very quickly to integrate XML into their products.

Oracle

Oracle (http://www.oracle.com) wants to lead the pack in the XML database arena. It released free XML components for all its development tools to allow the exchange of data between XML-formatted documents and Oracle databases without the need for third-party XML servers. Its XML Developer's Kit, which the company has been using internally to access the XML features of the Oracle8i database and Oracle Application Server, includes revised versions of Oracle's XML parser and XSL processor. All the parsers support both DOM and SAX interfaces.

Version 2.0 of Oracle's Java parser lets developers transform one XML document into another as well as convert a document from XML to other formats, such as HTML. It also allows extracting data from an XML document and saving it into an Oracle8i database in a single process.

Other components of the XML Developer's Kit include XML SQL Utilities which includes a converter between an XML document and HTML and XSQL Servlet which formats results from an SQL query as an XML document. The kit also contains both an XML class generator for creating XML documents from data and XML Transviewer Beans, a collection of JavaBeans components that lets any Java development environment work with XML documents.

eXcelon

Object Design Inc.'s eXcelon (http://objectdesign.com) is an XML application development environment for integrating data that uses XML as its native document format. It is an end-to-end solution positioned as a mid-tier server that can bridge the XML-based worlds of the Web and traditional databases allowing content owners to leverage information -- from the structured data in databases to semi structured and unstructured data in spreadsheets, COBOL files, documents, annotations, and Web pages. It provides a scalable middleware solution that improves data availability to applications and Web servers regardless of format.

eXcelon supports Microsoft Transaction Server and a development tool set for quickly enabling for XML legacy systems, enterprise resource planning systems, and other heterogeneous back-end data. It is an object-oriented database management system built on top of Object Design Inc.'s ObjectStore. Its strength is in ensuring the high availability of data resources.

eXcelon manages structured and unstructured information, allowing knowledge management systems to access and use any piece of knowledge, regardless of location or format. It also facilitates the personalization and customization of knowledge content, allowing information to be used in different ways depending on a user's context or requirements. It also enables continuous knowledge capture by allowing users to append information to documents and contribute content to the system dynamically.

eXcelon parses and stores data as XML to provide a hierarchy of persistent, discrete objects in its repository, the XMLStore. The store can then be indexed and queried using XQL. The results can then be customized and delivered through eXcelon's support of Java, Document Object Model, and Web server extensions. However, it has limited capabilities for validating XML and runs only on Windows NT.

eXcelon is particularly useful for product catalogs that contain large numbers of products, each with different attributes. For example, a monitor and a printer are both pieces of computer equipment; but each has very different marketing attributes. The monitor includes screen size and pixel resolution attributes. The printer, on the other hand, includes speed, footprint, and DPI resolution. A seller would also like to include marketing materials with each product, such as descriptions, pictures, and customer comments.

Product catalog data was formerly limited to a fixed set of identical attributes for all products. These attributes would include product name, stock number, price, etc. XML and eXcelon remove these constraints by allowing the combination and extension of structured data, like pricing and inventory data, with unstructured marketing & multimedia information such as descriptions, demos, and customer reviews. An eXcelon-based product catalog can accommodate new products and product attributes dynamically without disrupting service and without programming modifications.

The XQL Query Wizard provides an easy way to generate queries of the XMLStore and saves search time. The Studio offers a development environment for defining XML schemas which help hasten interface development to the XMLStore. It also provides several objects that allow accessing both the XQL query language and the XMLStore file system. A stand-alone tool, eXcelon Stylus, is a visual XSL editor. It offers an integrated view of XML data, an intelligent editing environment, and one-click visual debugging, making it quick and easy to deploy XML data on the Web.

ColdFusion

Allaire Corp. (http://www.allaire.com) is developing an XML-based add-on to its ColdFusion® Web Application Server that will let customers include e-commerce functions to their sites. The product, called Spectra, will permit adding metatag support to the ColdFusion Application Server. Spectra will let ColdFusion tackle e-commerce tasks that include procurement workflow, content management, transaction processing and personalization, giving buyers specific pricing.

POET's Content Management Suite (CMS) provides an open, scalable environment for the creation, management, and delivery of XML content. It is flexible enough to accommodate multiple DTDs, data types, applications, custom interfaces, legacy systems, and "best-of-breed" tools. It is able to check out content, track modifications and versions of documents, and check them in. It indexes documents at the component level and stores XML/SGML component "variants" for multiple languages. This lets users who work with multiple languages manage the process of translating, storing, and managing publications in several languages. CMS can store XML/SGML content in most European and Asian languages.

CMS comprises the following four components:

- Content Server which serves as a document repository and collaboration server.

- Content Server's FastObject™ architecture provides maximized component granularity, DTD flexibility, and multi-user performance.

- CMS Author Plug-ins which are tools for giving content contributors the ability to collaborate at the component level. POET Software is partnering with many other software producers to make Author Plug-ins available for popular XML and SGML authoring tools such as FrameMaker+SGML, Arbortext ADEPT Editor, Softquad's XmetaL, Allaire's ColdFusion,, and Ariba's cXML products.

- CMS Web Plug-in which uses templates and style sheets to deliver XML and SGML content dynamically to any web browser.

- Content SDK which is a collection of APIs-built upon POET FastObject™ technology-for plugging in best-of-breed tools, integrating with legacy systems, and creating custom user interfaces. It includes APIs for content management, version control, navigation, queries, database extensions, and embedding CMS ActiveX controls.

CMS, which is viewed as a Web-based server for technical and other complex documentation, runs on Windows NT 4.0, Windows 95, and Windows 98. The Content Server also runs on Solaris and HP-UX. It is built upon POET Object Server Suite (OSS), a high performance database for Java and C++ objects that helps manage the transfer of XML objects around the network. POET OSS enables the efficient delivery of complex data applications that perform better and require less coding and maintenance than applications built upon relational databases. It also has the flexibility and scalability for use in a wide variety of standalone, client/server, or multi-tier heterogeneous environments. Other major database players, such as Informix (with its product code-named CENTAUR), are also working to tie XML into object-relational database management systems (ORDBMSes).

Schemas

Commerce One's XML Development Kit is an XML schema toolkit that enables the creation of XML-based business documents and applications for an entire industry. The resulting XML-based applications will offer end users information-rich, robust e-commerce transactions that will become as ubiquitous as Web pages. Developers can download the XML Development Kit free of charge at Commerce One's MarketSite (http://www.marketsite.net).

Just as HTML provides ubiquitous communications for Web users, XML schemas provide the required structure and definition to enable buyers and suppliers to seamlessly conduct e-commerce on a global basis. The XML Development Kit lets developers create schemas to provide application-to-application interoperability. It also reduces application development time significantly by introducing object-oriented design for XML. In addition, it provides a powerful XML schema and DTD parser to validate XML documents; an industry standard SAX API set (Simple API for XML); and a rapid application development environment with strong data typing capabilities.

Commerce One's product line also includes Common Business Library, a set of XML schema components, documents, and a framework that allows the creation of robust, reusable, XML applications for e-commerce. It uses an open XML specification for an XML schema language that provides the framework for e-commerce transaction validation.

We mentioned Commerce One's liaisons with other agencies and organizations in establishing schemas in the previous chapter. There, we focused on efforts to promote the development of schemas for particular industries and their storage in repositories for general accessibility. Here, we focused on the tools Commerce One offers for developing schemas.

In this chapter, we concentrated on the different types of tools available specifically to create XML documents. We looked at four classes of tools: content development programs, application development packages, databases, and schema development kits. The list is not exhaustive, as it seems that new tools become available almost daily. The objective was to outline the most important classes of development tools and the questions to consider when selecting a tool for a particular purpose.

Bibliography

Abiteboul, Serge and Peter Buneman. *Data on the Web: From Relations to Semistructured Data and XML*. San Francisco: Morgan Kaufmann, 1999.

Boeri, Robert J. and Martin Hensel. XML: The New Document Standard. *Emedia Professional.* June 1998: 33.

Boumphrey, Frank. *Professional Style Sheets for HTML and XML*. Wrox Press Inc., 1999.

Boumphrey, Frank et al. *XML Applications*. Wrox Press Inc., 1998.

Bradley, Neil. *The XML Companion*. Harlow, England; Reading, MA: Addison-Wesley, c1998.

Ceponkus, Alex and Faraz Hoodbhoy. *XML Toolkit: A Toolkit for Programmers*. John Wiley, 1999.

Dalton, Gregory. XML On The Rise: Language Expected to Aid E-commerce, Help Web Searches. January 26, 1998. http://techweb.cmp.com/iw/666/66iuxml.htm

Drummond, Rik and Kay Spearman. XML Set to Change the Face of E-Commerce. *Network Computing.* May 1, 1998: 140-144.

DuCharme, Bob. *XML: The Annotated Specifications* (Charles F. Goldfarb Series on Open Information Management). Upper Saddle River, NJ: Prentice Hall Computer Books, 1999.

Goldfarb, Charles F., Steve Pepper, and Chet Ensign. *SGML Buyer's Guide : A Unique Guide to Determining Your Requirements and Choosing the Right SGML and XML Products and Services* (Charles F. Goldfarb Series). Upper Saddle River, NJ: Prentice Hall, 1998.

Goldfarb, Charles F. and Paul Prescod. *The XML Handbook.* Upper Saddle River, NJ: Prentice-Hall, 1998.

Gottesman, Ben Z. [et al.]. Why XML Matters. *PC Magazine.* October 6, 1998: 215-238.

Graham, Ian S. and Liam Quin. *XML Specification Guide.* John Wiley & Sons, 1999.

Guidelines for using XML for Electronic Data Interchange. Version 0.05. Martin Bryan, Editor. January 25, 1998. http://www.geocities.com/WallStreet/Floor/5815/guide.htm

Harold, Elliotte Rusty. *XML: Extensible Markup Language.* Foster City, CA: IDG Books Worldwide, 1998.

Heid, Jim. XML Spoken Here: New Web Language Promises Smarter Surfing. *PC World.* August 1998: 70.

Holzner, Steven. *XML Complete* (McGraw-Hill Complete Series). New York: Computing McGraw-Hill, 1997.

Hoque, Reaz. *XML for Real Programmers.* San Francisco: Morgan Kaufmann, 1999.

Hurley, Hanna. EDI Takes to the Internet. *Network Magazine.* October 1998: 36-40.

Jelliffe, Richard A. *The XML and SGML Cookbook : Recipes for Structured Information* (Charles F. Goldfarb Series). Upper Saddle River, NJ: Prentice Hall, 1999.

Kerstetter, Jim. XML Holds Promise as EDI Replacement. *PC Week.* May 1, 1998.

Klinger, Steven P. XML Expands Web App Possibilities. *LANTimes.* June 8, 1998: 26.

Krantz, Michael. Keeping Tabs Online: Doing Business on the Net is Hard Because the Underlying Software is so Dumb; XML Will Fix That (new markup language). *Time* 150:20 (November 10, 1997) pp. 81ss.

Leventhal, Michael, David Lewis, and Matthew Fuchs. *Designing XML Internet Applications*. Upper Saddle River, NJ: Prentice-Hall, 1998.

Levitt, Jason. The Making of a Markup Language. *Information Week*. May 25, 1998: 70-80.

Light, Richard. *Presenting XML*. Indianapolis: Sams.net, 1997.

Marchal, Benoît. *Electronic Data Interchange on The Internet*. http://developer.netscape.com/viewsource/marchal_edata.htm

Markup and Metadata. *Digital Publishing Technologies*. April 1998: 11-16.

McGrath, Sean. *XML by Example: Building E-Commerce Applications*. Upper Saddle River, NJ: Prentice-Hall, 1998.

Megginson, David. *Structuring XML Documents*. Upper Saddle River, NJ: Prentice-Hall, 1998.

Messmer, Ellen. Software Aims to Bridge EDI/XML Traffic. *Network World*. July 13, 1998: 6.

Millman, Howard. A Brief History of EDI. *Infoworld.* April 6, 1998: 83.

North, Simon and Paul Hermans. *Sams Teach Yourself XML in 21 Days*. Indianapolis, IN: Sams, 1999.

Pardi, William J. *XML in Action*. Redmond, WA: Microsoft Press, 1999.

Rist, Oliver. XML Comes of Age. *Internet Week*. August 16, 1999: 31-36.

Simpson, John C. *Just XML*. Upper Saddle River, NJ: Prentice-Hall, 1998.

Sinclair, Joseph T. *SMIL & Streaming Media for Webmasters*. San Francisco: Morgan Kaufmann, 1999.

Smith, Norman E. *Practical Guide to SGML/XML Filters*. Wordware Publishing, 1998.

Spencer, Paul. *XML Design and Implementation*. Wrox Press Inc., 1999.

St. Laurent, Simon and Ethan Cerami. *Building XML Applications*. New York: McGraw-Hill, 1999.

St. Laurent, Simon and Robert J. Biggar. *Inside XML DTDs: Scientific and Technical*. New York: McGraw-Hill, 1999.

St. Laurent. Simon. *XML: A Primer*. Foster City, CA: MIS Press, 1998.

Stanek, William Robert. PC Labs Reviews. *PC Magazine*. October 6, 1998. http://www.zdnet.com/pcmag/features/xml98/xml201.html

Stanek, William Robert. Structuring Data With XML Extensible Markup Language Lets Developers Describe Virtually Any Type of Data and Deliver It Across a Network. *PC Magazine.* May 26, 1998. http://www.zdnet.com/pcmag/pctech/content/17/10/tf1710.001.html

Swenson, John. XML: A Better Way to Move Data Across the Web. *MSDN Online*. January 21, 1998. http://www.microsoft.com/msdn/news/imho/012198.htm

Tittel, Ed, Norbert Mikula, and Ramesh Norbert. *XML for Dummies*. Foster City, CA: IDG Books Worldwide, 1998.

Udell, Jon. XML Describes Structured Data Packages That Move Around the Web as Easily as HTML. *Byte.* 23 (January 1998): 80. http://www.byte.com/art/9801/sec5/art18.htm

Web Sites

Allaire: http://www.allaire.com

Ariba: http://corp.ariba.com/corp/Home/default.asp

Biztalk: http://www.biztalk.org

Bluestone Software: http://www.bluestone.com

CommerceNet: http://www.commercenet.com

Commerce One: http://www.commerceone.com

cXML.org: http://www.cxml.org/home

DataChannel: http://www.datachannel.com

Datastream: http://www.dstm.com

Enigma: http://www.enigmainc.com

Extricity: http://www.extricity.com

IBM's XML site: http://www.software.ibm.com

IBM's developer site: http://www.ibm.com/developer/xml

Microsoft's XML site: http://msdn.microsoft.com/xml

Microstar: http://www.microstar.com

OBI Consortium: http://www.openbuy.org

Object Design: http://www.odi.com/excelon/Main.htm

Open Applications Group: http://www.openapplications.org

Oracle: http://www.oracle.com

Robin Cover's SGML/XML Web Page: http://www.oasis-open.org/cover

RosettaNet: http://www.rosettanet.org

Sequoia: http://www.sequoiasw.com/index.htm

Software AG: http://www.softwareag.com

Sun Microsystems: http://www.sun.com

Sybase: http://www.sybase.com

Vignette: http://www.vignette.com

World Wide Web Committee: http://www.w3.org

XML.com: http://www.xml.com

XML/EDI Group: http://www.xmledi.net

XML.org: http://www.xml.org

XMLINFO: http://www.xmlinfo.com (links to XML tutorials, books, conferences, etc.)

XML Repository: http://www.xmlrepository.com

XML Resources Page http://www.infoworld.com/xml

World Wide Web Consortium: http://www.w3.org

Mailing Lists

XML-L: listserv.headnet.ie/cgi-bin/wa?A0=xml-l (good mailing list for XML novices)

XML-dev: http://www.lists.ic.ac.uk/hypermail/xml-dev

Glossary

absolute addressing: XPointers which refer to a specific occurrence of some piece of the element tree, usually by using an ID, are said to use absolute addressing.

action: The portion of a rule which defines the style characteristics to be applied to the pattern. In XSL, the second part of a style rule defines the style or styles to apply to the element identified by the selection part of the rule.

agent: A program that operates on a user's behalf, performing its task in the background and delivering results at the end of its task.

ancestor and descendant elements: Any element which contains another element no matter how many intervening levels separate them in an ancestor element. Any element which is contained within another element is a descendant element. Immediate ancestors and descendants are thus parent and children, respectively. For example, a Book element would be the ancestor of a Paragraph and also of the Chapter containing the Paragraph.

anchor: A tag embedded in the text that serves as the source of a hypertext link. The link is "anchored" because it stays with the relevant text if it is moved due to insertions or deletions earlier in the document.

API: Application Program Interface. A specification for the interface of a software package by which other programs can utilize that package. An XML processor must have an API through which applications can receive XML data.

applet: A self-contained program that runs in a specific environment, usually a Web browser.

application: A piece of software on behalf of which an XML processor processes XML documents. More generally, a usage of the generic XML framework for a particular purpose, with its own DTD, linking conventions, and style sheets.

arc: A connection between two nodes.

ASCII (American Standard Code for Information Interchange): A coding method to translate characters, such as numbers, text, and symbols, into digital form.

attribute: Various properties that modify or refine the meaning of an element and consist of a name and a value. The attribute is named to distinguish it from other attributes and values in the same element. Some tags take required attributes, some have optional attributes, and some have both types. Attribute values can be specified in the element's start tag or default values can be inherited from the DTD.

attribute declaration: A declaration in a DTD specifying an attribute's name, type, and default value, if any.

attribute list declaration: The markup used to define attributes and assign them to a specific element. It contains the element's name and any restrictions on its value.

binary entity: An entity with content that is either not XML format, or is XML but is not to be parsed as part of the document. It must be an external entity. Typically used for image data. See parsed entity.

cascade: Refers to the hierarchy of "decisions" about how a Web page's components should look.

cascading style sheets (CSS): A style sheet language to define how certain HTML, DHTML, or XML structural elements (paragraphs, headings, etc.) should be displayed.

CDATA section: A part of an XML document in which markup (apart from that indicating the en d of the CDATA [non-parsed character data] section) is not interpreted as markup, but is passed to the application as is.

CGI (Common Gateway Interface): A standard that allows programs of various types to interact with Web servers, usually to provide interactive response to user input from a browser.

channel: Information about organized content on an intranet or the Internet.

character: A letter, digit, or symbol represented within a computer by a numeric code.

character data: The actual text of an XML document, as opposed to the markup of the document.

character entities: Strings of characters that represent other characters.

character reference: An escape code for a single Unicode character that quotes the numerical value of its bit string.

child element: An element enclosed in another element. Child elements may contain children of their own.

client: An application that requests services from a server application. Any software that uses the Document Object Model programming interfaces provided by the hosting implementation to accomplish useful work.

comment: A piece of markup within an XML document containing text that is not to be treated as part of the document.

conditional section: In the DTD, a piece of markup that can be included in, or excluded from, the logical structure of the DTD, depending on the keyword at its start.

connector: The part of a locator (# or |) that separates the URL from an XPointer. The # symbol tells the agent to process the XPointer while the | symbol tells the server to perform this action.

construction rules: One of two kinds of rules that may be used in XSL, a construction rule creates flow objects. It specifies a pattern and construction of an element (for example, constructing a division using the <DIV>...</DIV> tags when the specified pattern is found. The other kind of rule is style rules.

content model: The grammar governing the allowed types of the child elements and the order in which they appear. In the DTD, a description of what might occur within instances of a given element type. It shows what sort(s) of content an element may contain: parsed character data and/or other elements; and, if the latter, which elements it may contain; how many times they may occur in the context of the element; and in what order they must appear.

content-identifier: A token that can be used to uniquely identify any piece of data or content.

core flow objects: The flow objects defined under the HTML/CSS2 and DSSL standards for use in XSL.

data model: A data model is a collection of descriptions of data structures and their contained fields, together with the operations or functions that manipulate the model.

delimiter set: An SGML declaration instruction that is used to assign different strings and characters that have the same semantics as the characters found in HTML.

descendant: An element that is enclosed either directly or indirectly by another element. See ancestor and descendant.

document: see XML document

Document Character Set: An SGML declaration instruction that allows users to specify which character set to use in a document. XML uses the ISO/IEC 10646 character set, which is similar to Unicode.

document element: The first element in a document. The single element that contains all the other elements and character data that make up an XML document, also known as the root element.

document type declaration: A declaration at the start of an XML document that specifies where the exter nal DTD subset can be found and includes the internal DTD subset. In valid documents, the declaration that connects a document to its DTD.

document type definition: see DTD

DOM (Document Object Model): A platform- and language-neutral program interface that allows programs and scripts to access and update the content, structure, and style of documents in a standard way.

DSSSL: Document Style Semantics and Specification Language. A transformation and style language for the processing and formatting of valid SGML documents. The parent language from which XSL is derived.

DSSSL-o: A subset of DSSSL, called the online profile, proposed as a cut-down version of DSSL suitable for rendering XML documents.

DTD: A set of rules governing the structure and element content of an XML document and specifying the content and attributes of each element type. The DTD also declares all the external entities referenced within the document and the notations that can be used. See also external DTD subset.

EDI: Electronic Data Interchange. The exchange of structured business information by electronic means.

electronic commerce: The exchange of money and goods over the Internet or some other public network.

element: The fundamental logical unit of information within an XML document. All content in XML documents must be contained within elements. Elements may contain other elements, processing instructions, actual text, etc.

element construction rule: An instruction in an XSL stylesheet that specifies which flow objects are to be constructed when a particular element type is encountered.

element content: In a DTD, a content model that allows other elements only inside instances of a given element type. (Compare with mixed content.)

element type: A particular type of element, such as a paragraph. An element's type is indicated by the name that occurs in its start tag and end tag.

empty element: An element that has no textual content. An empty tag is usually used to signal to the processing software some condition inherent in the tag itself.

encoding declaration: A declaration of the character encoding scheme used for a particular text entity.

end tag: A tag that marks the end of an element, such as </section>.

entity: Any data that can be treated as an object, such as an external file containing an image. An entity refers to other data that often acts as an abbreviation or a shortcut.

entity declaration: Part of the DTD. An entity declaration declares a name for an entity and associates it with a replacement string or externally stored data identified by a URL.

entity reference: A reference within the text of an XML document to a previously declared entity, signifying that the contents of the entity are to be processed at this point (processing can also mean simple inclusion).

extended link: A link that contains locator elements. It can involve any number of resources. An extended link doesn't need to be co-located with any of the resources involved in the link. Compare with simple link.

extended link group: A group of documents whose contents are analyzed for links to help establish two-way links without requiring their declaration in every document.

Extended Pointer: see XPointer

external DTD subset: The part of the DTD that is stored outside of the document. The external DTD subset is often referred to as the DTD of a class of documents because it is convenient for storing DTD that will be used by multiple documents. See also DTD.

external entity: An entity whose contents are contained in an external XML resource, such as an image file, referred to from within an XML document.

external text entity: An entity held in a separate file (an external entity) that contains XML data to be parsed and merged-in to the document.

flow object: A formatting feature, such as a paragraph or a table cell, into which the content of an XML document is flowed under the control of an XSL style sheet.

flow object tree: The complete set of flow objects into which an XML document is converted by an XSL stylesheet.

frames: A way of dividing Web pages into multiple regions that can be scrolled independently.

generic entities: Entities used to supply boilerplate or other commonly used text in an XML document.

generic identifier: The name assigned to an element type.

grove: Graph Representation of property ValuEs. A representation of an XML document in which each node represents a property of the document.

GUI (Graphical User Interface): A computer interface in which windows, graphics, and a mouse (or trackball) are used to interact with information instead of plain text at a command line.

hosting implementation: A software module that provides an implementation of the DOM interfaces so that a client application can use them. Some examples of hosting implementations are browsers, editors, and document repositories.

hot spot: An area of a graphical image that acts as a link to associated information when selected.

HTML: HyperText Markup Language. An encoding scheme for displaying and hyperlinking pages of information on the World Wide Web. Some versions of HTML are applications of SGML.

HTML syntax: The rules that govern the construction of intelligible HTML documents or markup fragments.

hypertext: Text that does not follow a single narrative flow. A way of linking document locations together so that when a particular element is clicked, the user is taken to another location within the same document or to another Web document.

HyTime: Hypermedia/Time-based Structuring Language (ISO/IEC 10744-1992). An SGML application that extends SGML capabilities to allow such things as multimedia capabilities and advanced linking extensions to SGML. One of the foundations of XLink.

inline: 1. An object that is embedded in a sequence of other objects, such as a paragraph element that follows and precedes similar text structures. See out-of-line. 2. An element that identifies a hypertext link which is embedded with the referencing text.

inline link: See simple link

inline styles: A style that applies to an element within the XML document itself.

internal DTD subset: The part of the DTD that is declared within the XML document itself before the first start tag.

internal entity: An entity whose value is given in its entity declaration in the DTD.

internal text entity: A text entity that includes the replacement text inside the entity declaration. See external text entity.

interpret: The step-by-step process of a software application that reads a data file containing instructions that are mainly designed to be human legible. This is a slow process and must be repeated each time the file is read.

interpreter: A module of a larger program that needs to read data designed to be also human-readable.

Java: A multi-platform object-oriented programming language that is used for Web application development. It was created by Sun Microsystems in 1992 for use in consumer devices. In 1995, it was enhanced and aimed at Internet applications.

JPEG: (pronounced "jay-peg") A 24-bit raster image format that uses an efficient compression scheme. It is a "lossy" format as it does not faithfully reproduce the original image. Used in preference to GIF for natural color images, primarily photographs.

keyword: A word apearing in markup that identifies the purpose of the tag, or some part of it.

link: The information about both the local and remote resources to establish a hyperlink as well as the characteristics of the link.

link feature: An SGML feature that lets users add formatting instructions -- or other associations for some element -- without altering the document's content.

linking element: An element that contains an attribute that identifies another resource.

location source: The point where some particular portion of a relatively-addressed XPointer begins. Originally, it is the root element; but as the XPointer successively selects children, descendants, strings, etc., the location source changes with each "move."

locator: A locator is essentially a URL, i.e. a designator for where on the Web a remote resource can be found. A character string that identifies one end of a link.

logical structure: The declarations, elements, character references, processing instructions, and so on that make up an XML document. These are all indicated by explicit markup.

macro: A text or code script that performs an action when called, usually used to automate repetitive keystrokes and/or mouse click sequences.

markup: Structural information stored in the same file as the content. This information indicates the document's logical and physical structure.

markup declaration: A special tag in XML that is not used to mark-up a document but is used for many other purposes, such as to build the document structure rules (the DTD), identify and locate each entity or define alternative document segments.

metadata: Data about data, existing only to identify or describe some information. Specially defined elements that describe a document's structure, content, or rendering, within the document itself, or through external references.

metalanguage: A language used to communicate information about language itself; many experts consider both SGML and XML to be metalanguages because they can be used to define markup languages.

MIME: (Multi-purpose Independent Mail Extensions). A standard for identifying the formats in a mixed media mail or HTTP message, including pictures and text.

mixed content: Elements that may contain both other elements and character data of their own.

model: The data representation for the information at hand. Examples are the structural model and the style model representing the parse structure and the style information associated with a document. The model might be a tree or a graph or something else.

multiway links: Special-purpose hyperlinks in an XML document where a single link can simultaneously point to multiple targets. On a multi-frame page, this would allow a single hyperlink to cause multiple frame areas to be updated at the same time.

name: Within an XML DTD, a letter or underscore followed by zero or more name characters.

name character: A letter, digit, hyphen, underscore, period, colon, or one of a set of special characters specified in the XML standard. These characters can be used in the names of XML elements, attributes, and other key identifiers.

name token: Any mixture of name characters.

named style: A set of style characteristics that is given a name for use in either construction rules or style rules under XSL.

namespace: A method for qualifying the names used in XML documents by associating them with contexts identified by URIs.

nested element: An element that may contain itself, directly, or indirectly via another element, thus allowing potentially endless recursion.

node: An object in a grove, consisting of at least one property. An element definition in a DTD can be represented by a node, with properties for its attribute definitions and its content model.

non-parsed character data: See CDATA section.

non-validating XML processor: An XML processor that checks whether XML documents are well-formed but not whether they are valid.

normalization: When minimization has been used in a document, normalization is the process of inserting the missing markup.

normalized space: To separate terms in various contexts, it is sufficient to insert a single space character between they, yet DTD and document authors may use other white space characters or multiple spaces. An XML processor reduces a sequence of white space characters to a single space.

notation: Specification for the processing of external binary entities. It tells an XML application which outside program to invoke to handle content of a given media type, such as a GIF image or an MPEG video, that the XML processor does not "understand."

notation declaration: A declaration that assigns a unique name to a non-XML format and may identify a document describing the format and/or a program capable of processing the format.

object: An identifiable unit of information, possibly containing both discrete data units and also functions that operate on that data.

object model: A collection of descriptions of classes or interfaces together with their member data, member functions, and class-static operations.

occurrence/instance: An occurrence or instance refers to the number of times some bit of content may appear in an element's content model.

out-of-line: An object that is not part of a sequence of objects, such as paragraphs on a page. Used to describe a type of hypertext link where the element that describes the link is not embedded in the text. See in-line.

out-of-line link: A link that includes no information about the local resource. This type of link can even appear in separate files. It allows developers to declare links separately from the content of the document.

parameter: Feature of a tag that can contain modifying variables. A parameter value may have a meaning associated with its location in the tag or indicated by a parameter name. An attribute is an XML element parameter, and each attribute has a name and a value.

parameter entity: A text entity used within a DTD or used to control processing of conditional sections. It is used to represent information within the context of a DTD and may be used to link the content of additional DTD files to a DTD. Used to aid construction of a DTD.

parameter entity reference: An entity reference that can be entered only within markup, so is mostly the province of the DTD author rather than the document author.

parent and child elements: A parent element is the containing element immediately above any other element or piece of content in the element tree. A child element is any element immediately below some other element in the element tree. All elements in the element tree, except the root element, are children.

parse: Decoding and understanding, using the rules of a grammar. In XML, the process of checking the legal use of markup, as performed by the validating parser module of an XML processor.

parsed character data: Text that will be examined by the parser for entities and markup.

parsed entity: An entity whose content is valid XML data, forming part of the document structure, so is required to be parsed by any validating parser. See binary entity.

parser: XML processing software which 1. determines whether a document is valid or well-formed, and 2. passes a stream of "correct" XML to an application, such as a browser. The parser may take various corrective actions if it encounters problems with the code.

pattern: The portion of an XSL rule which identifies the subset of the target XML document to which a style is to be applied.

physical structure: The arrangement of physical storage units (entities) in which an XML document is held.

PICS (Platform for Internet Content Selection) label: PICS labels are used to give better control over the content that can be accessed by certain audiences.

port: A communication channel through which an Internet application sends or receives data.

presentation markup tag: A tag that affects a document's display characteristics.

primary key: An element's unique identifier.

priority attribute: An XSL attribute that contributes to defining the specificity of a style rule against competing rules. When all other factors are equal, the rule with the higher priority value wins.

procedural markup: A markup scheme that describes how a document should look, possibly including font descriptions and character styles, such as roman and italic.

processing instruction (PI): A piece of markup that gives information or instructions to software that will process an XML document. A PI does not form part of the document's character data.

prolog: The optional part of an XML document that precedes the root element. It may include the XML declaration itself, the document type declaration, comments, and processing instructions.

property: One piece of information in an object. The part of a CSS rule which identifies the style characteristics such as font size, position on the page, margins, etc. that are to be applied to the rule's selector.

public identifier: An external entity identifier that is not system specific (in terms of identifying either format or entity location). This identifier is expected to be compared with an entry in a catalog file which provides the location and name of the system file.

quadding: In XSL, a characteristic of paragraph that gives the alignment of the text, 'start' (left justified in English left-to-right mode) 'end' (right justified in English) or 'center'.

query language: A computer language designed for the purpose of requesting information from a database. A request formed in such a language is called a query.

RDBMS (Relational Database Management System): A table-oriented database management system built around the relational model first developed at IBM in the 1970s by E. F. Codd and C. J. Date. Microsoft Access, Sybase SQL Server, and Oracle are all relational database systems.

RDF (Resource Description Framework): An effort from the W3C to consolidate and coordinate many related efforts to define metadata that can describe what documents contain (or what they can deliver) using consistent, coherent markup and notation.

relative addressing: If an XPointer refers to some sub-resource by "walking the element tree" -- i.e. by locating the target resource relative to other pieces of the element tree that you're not interested in -- it is using relative addressing.

relative link: A hypertext link that identifies the location of a resource in relation to some other resource, typically the location of the source document or element.

relative location: A hypertext link target that is not identified by a unique code, but by its location relative to other elements. For example, a link could be made to the fifth paragraph in the third chapter of a document.

rendering: The act of processing a document so that it can be viewed. Rendering normally implies display on a screen but could also mean other forms of processing, such as text-to-speech conversion for the blind.

reserved attribute: An attribute name that cannot be defined for ad hoc use by DTD authors because it has special significance in all XML applications. All reserved attributes begin with "xml."

resource: An object that is the target of a hypertext link. Any addressable unit of in formation that can be involved in a link. A resource can include complete XML documents, HTML documents, images, elements (or spans of elements) within them, and chunks of text.

root element: See document element

SAX (Simple API for XML): A proposal for a standard interface to XML parsers from object oriented programs. Includes a number of classes.

schema: A pattern that represents the data's model defining the elements (or objects), their attributes (or properties), and the relationships between the different elements.

scripting: Creating a set of instructions for a Web page using a scripting language.

scripting language: A specialized programming language used to create scripts that, when inserted into a Web page, control various elements of the page, such as the user interface, styles, and HTML markup.

separator: One or more characters used within a defined context to separate objects, such as one markup parameter from another.

SGML: Standard Generalized Markup Language. An International Standard (ISO 8879:1986) that describes a generalized markup scheme for representing the logical structure of documents in a system- and platform-independent manner. The parent language of XML.

SGML declaration: Contains certain instructions, independent of a DTD, for an SGML parser.

sibling elements: Any two elements which share the same parent.

significant white space: Spaces, tabs, and line break codes which are considered to be part of the document text, so should be preserved and appear when the document is presented.

simple element: The name of the XLL element that identifies the source of a hypertext link that has a single target resource.

simple link: An inline link, such as the familiar <A HREF=""> tag in HTML, that links a specific point in an XML document to some target. Describes the local and remote resources of an XLink. Compare with extended link.

SMIL (Synchronized Multimedia Integration Language): A language designed to allow the integration of a collection of multimedia objects in a synchronized fashion for presentation over the Web.

start tag: A tag that marks the start of an element, such as <para>.

style rule: A style rule specifies a pattern and an action that the rule applies directly to the targeted portion of the document when the pattern is found. It does not create flow objects from the target XML document, unlike a construction rule.

style sheet: A file that holds the layout settings for a certain category of documents. Style sheets, like templates, contain settings for headers and footers, tabs, margins, fonts, columns, etc.

Stylesheet Object Model: Cascading Style Sheets (CSS) is one model for manipulating style in a document. The Stylesheet Object Model exposes the ability to create, modify, and associate CSS stylesheets with documents.

syntax: The rules of grammar that define a language. The XML syntax defines how tags and markup declarations are stored and identified.

tag: A code embedded in the text signifying the structure, format, or style of the data. Except for empty tags, tags must always occur in pairs, surrounding the content they are meant to mark up.

target: The object of a hypertext link. It must be identified by a unique name or code which can be used within a source object to form the link.

target element: An XSL element that identifies the element to be styled in the action part of the style rule.

TEI (Text Encoding Initiative): A compact syntax for creating complex links. TEI is one of the standards that influenced the design of the XML eXtensible Linking Language (XLL). TEI's guidelines furnish a concise syntax for designating complicated links.

token: A single unit of text separated from other tokens by white space. Roughly analogous to a "word."

transclusion: A hypertext concept that involves replacing the source reference with the target resource. The link is not so much followed as brought to the reference. An ideal mechanism for ensuring that a reference to a title is always accurate.

traversal: Use of a link to access the resource at its other (or another) end. For simple links, traversal can be thought of as the action of following a link.

tree: A hierarchical structure which resembles a tree in that the structure can be viewed as branches. SGML elements form hierarchies and are sometimes described using the family tree concept, including the use of names such as ancestor, parent, child, sibling.

Unicode character set: A 16-bit character encoding scheme defined in ISO/IED 10646 that encompasses standard Roman and Greek alphabets, plus mathematical symbols, special punctuation, and non-Roman alphabets that include Hebrew, Chinese, Arabic, Hanggul, and others.

URI (Uniform Resource Identifier): A character string that identifies the type and location of an Internet resource.

URL (Uniform Resource Locator): Subset of the URI protocol for addressing information on the Web.

valid XML document: An XML document is valid if its structure and element content are formally declared in a DTD. A well-formed document that also conforms to all the rules governing the structure of its content expressed in its DTD.

validating parser: A parser that compares the usage of elements and attributes in a document against the rules of a DTD.

W3C: World Wide Web Consortium. A group of vendor companies that acts as a sort of standards body for the Web.

Web: A common name for the World Wide Web. An Internet service that uses the HTTP protocol and the HTML format to deliver documents.

well-formed XML document: An XML document is well formed if it does not require a DTD to understand its structure and element content and it still complies with general XML principles such as proper tag nesting.

white space: A character used to separate words in text and parameters in markup, including the space character, the horizontal tab character, and end-of-line codes.

XLL (eXtensible Linking Language): In XML documents, it is a language that provides a simple set of instructions that describe the links among objects. It also maintains the addressing inside XML documents.

XML: eXtensible Markup Language. A profile, or simplified subset, of SGML. A system for defining, validating, and sharing document formats.

XML declaration: A processing instruction at the start of an XML document that declares it to be XML code.

XML dialect: Any implementation of domain-specific XML notation governed by a standard DTD designed to support chemical markup (CML), mathematical markup (MathML), channel definitions (CDF), and so forth.

XML document: A "textual object." A document consists of an optional XML declaration, followed by an optional document type declaration, and then followed by a document element.

XML processor: A program that reads XML documents, checks whether they are valid and well-formed, and makes their contents available to XML applications.

XPointer: A syntax for identifying the element, range of elements, or text within an XML document that is the target resource of a link.

XSL: The XML style language. As CSS, it defines the specification for an XML document's presentation and appearance. Both CSS and XSL provide a platform-independent method for specifying the document's presentation style.

Appendix 1

Library of Congress' SGML Format

An example of a MARC DTD that defines USMARC data in SGML format. Note the use of Chinese characters. The machine readable code for these symbols uses Unicode, an extension of ASCII to accommodate non-roman characters. An XML-aware browser, like Internet Explorer 5, displays these characters in proper fashion.

Library of Congress' SGML Format: An Example

```
<mrcb format-type="bd">
<mrcbldr-bd>
<mrcbldr-bd-05 value="n">
<mrcbldr-bd-06 value="a">
<mrcbldr-bd-07 value="m">
<mrcbldr-bd-08 value="blank">
<mrcbldr-bd-09 value="blank">
<mrcbldr-bd-17 value="blank">
<mrcbldr-bd-18 value="a">
<mrcbldr-bd-19 value="blank">
</mrcbldr-bd>
<mrcb-control-fields>
<mrcb001>AAEX</mrcb001>
<mrcb001>2127507</mrcb001>
<mrcb008-bk>
<mrcb008-bk-00-05 value="980627">
<mrcb008-bk-06 value="n">
<mrcb008-bk-07-10 value="blank">
<mrcb008-bk-11-14 value="blank">
<mrcb008-bk-15-17 value="ch ">
<mrcb008-bk-18-21 value="blank">
<mrcb008-bk-22 value="blank">
<mrcb008-bk-23 value="blank">
<mrcb008-bk-24-27 value="blank">
<mrcb008-bk-28 value="blank">
<mrcb008-bk-29 value="0">
<mrcb008-bk-30 value="0">
<mrcb008-bk-31 value="0">
<mrcb008-bk-32 value="blank">
<mrcb008-bk-33 value="0">
<mrcb008-bk-34 value="blank">
<mrcb008-bk-35-37 value="chi">
<mrcb008-bk-38 value="blank">
<mrcb008-bk-39 value="d">
</mrcb008-bk>
<mrcb008-bk>
<mrcb008-bk-00-05 value="920811">
<mrcb008-bk-06 value="s">
<mrcb008-bk-07-10 value="1991">
<mrcb008-bk-11-14 value="blank">
<mrcb008-bk-15-17 value="ch ">
<mrcb008-bk-18-21 value="blank">
<mrcb008-bk-22 value="blank">
<mrcb008-bk-23 value="blank">
<mrcb008-bk-24-27 value="b   ">
<mrcb008-bk-28 value="blank">
<mrcb008-bk-29 value="0">
```

```
<mrcb008-bk-30 value="0">
<mrcb008-bk-31 value="0">
<mrcb008-bk-32 value="blank">
<mrcb008-bk-33 value="0">
<mrcb008-bk-34 value="blank">
<mrcb008-bk-35-37 value="chi">
<mrcb008-bk-38 value="blank">
<mrcb008-bk-39 value="d">
</mrcb008-bk>
</mrcb-control-fields>
<mrcb-numbers-and-codes>
<mrcb020 i1="i1-blank" i2="i2-blank">
<mrcb020-a>9571502537 (deluxe e</mrcb020-a>
</mrcb020>
<mrcb020 i1="i1-blank" i2="i2-blank">
<mrcb020-a>9571502545 (pbk.)</mrcb020-a>
</mrcb020>
<mrcb040 i1="i1-blank" i2="i2-blank">
<mrcb040-a>GZM</mrcb040-a>
<mrcb040-c>GZM</mrcb040-c>
<mrcb040-d>HNK</mrcb040-d>
</mrcb040>
<mrcb090 i1="i1-blank" i2="i2-blank">
<mrcb090-a>PL2470.Z6</mrcb090-a>
<mrcb090-b>C467 1991</mrcb090-b>
</mrcb090>
</mrcb-numbers-and-codes>
<mrcb-main-entry>
<mrcb100 i1="i1-1" i2="i2-blank">
<mrcb100-a>程元敏.</mrcb100-a>
</mrcb100>
<mrcb100 i1="i1-1" i2="i2-blank">
<mrcb100-a>Cheng, Yuan-min.</mrcb100-a>
</mrcb100>
</mrcb-main-entry>
<mrcb-title-and-title-related>
<mrcb245 i1="i1-1" i2="i2-0">
<mrcb245-a>春秋左氏經傳集解序疏證 /</mrcb245-a>
<mrcb245-c>程元敏著.</mrcb245-c>
</mrcb245>
<mrcb245 i1="i1-1" i2="i2-0">
<mrcb245-a>Chun chiu Tso shih ching chuan chi chieh hsu shu cheng /</mrcb245-a>
<mrcb245-c>Cheng Yuan-min chu.</mrcb245-c>
</mrcb245>
<mrcb250 i1="i1-blank" i2="i2-blank">
<mrcb250-a>初版.</mrcb250-a>
</mrcb250>
<mrcb250 i1="i1-blank" i2="i2-blank">
<mrcb250-a>Chu pan.</mrcb250-a>
</mrcb250>
</mrcb-title-and-title-related>
```

```
<mrcb-edition-imprint-etc>
<mrcb260 i1="i1-blank" i2="i2-blank">
<mrcb260-a>臺北市 :</mrcb260-a>
<mrcb260-b>臺灣學生書局,</mrcb260-b>
<mrcb260-c>民國80 [1991]</mrcb260-c>
</mrcb260>
<mrcb260 i1="i1-blank" i2="i2-blank">
<mrcb260-a>Tai-pei shih :</mrcb260-a>
<mrcb260-b>Tai-wan hsueh sheng shu chu,</mrcb260-b>
<mrcb260-c>Min kuo 80 [1991]</mrcb260-c>
</mrcb260>
</mrcb-edition-imprint-etc>
<mrcb-physical-description>
<mrcb300 i1="i1-blank" i2="i2-blank">
<mrcb300-a>112 p. ;</mrcb300-a>
<mrcb300-c>22 cm.</mrcb300-c>
</mrcb300>
</mrcb-physical-description>
<mrcb-notes>
<mrcb504 i1="i1-blank" i2="i2-blank">
<mrcb504-a>Includes bibliographical references (p. 109-112)</mrcb504-a>
</mrcb504>
</mrcb-notes>
<mrcb-subject-access>
<mrcb600 i1="i1-0" i2="i2-0">
<mrcb600-a>孔子.</mrcb600-a>
<mrcb600-t>春秋.</mrcb600-t>
</mrcb600>
<mrcb600 i1="i1-0" i2="i2-0">
<mrcb600-a>Confucius.</mrcb600-a>
<mrcb600-t>Chun chiu.</mrcb600-t>
</mrcb600>
<mrcb600 i1="i1-2" i2="i2-0">
<mrcb600-a>左丘明.</mrcb600-a>
<mrcb600-t>左傳.</mrcb600-t>
</mrcb600>
<mrcb600 i1="i1-2" i2="i2-0">
<mrcb600-a>Tso-chiu, Ming.</mrcb600-a>
<mrcb600-t>Tso chuan.</mrcb600-t>
</mrcb600>
</mrcb-subject-access>
<mrcb-added-entry>
<mrcb700 i1="i1-2" i2="i2-2">
<mrcb700-a>左丘明.</mrcb700-a>
<mrcb700-t>左傳.</mrcb700-t>
<mrcb700-f>1991.</mrcb700-f>
</mrcb700>
<mrcb700 i1="i1-2" i2="i2-2">
<mrcb700-a>Tso-chiu, Ming.</mrcb700-a>
<mrcb700-t>Tso chuan.</mrcb700-t>
<mrcb700-f>1991.</mrcb700-f>
```

```
</mrcb700>
<mrcb700 i1="i1-0" i2="i2-2">
<mrcb700-a>孔子.</mrcb700-a>
<mrcb700-t>春秋.</mrcb700-t>
<mrcb700-f>1991.</mrcb700-f>
</mrcb700>
<mrcb700 i1="i1-0" i2="i2-2">
<mrcb700-a>Confucius.</mrcb700-a>
<mrcb700-t>Chun chiu.</mrcb700-t>
<mrcb700-f>1991.</mrcb700-f>
</mrcb700>
</mrcb-added-entry>
</mrcb>
```

Appendix 2

Bibliographic Record in XML Format

This example shows how the bibliographic data in Appendix 1 might look in an OPAC. The first instance shows the bibliographic record without the Chinese characters. The second instance displays the same record but with the Chinese characters encoded in BIG5 instead of the default encoding scheme, Unicode (UTF-8). An XML-aware browser, like Internet Explorer 5, will understand both of these encoding schemes and display non-roman characters in proper fashion.

Coded by K. T. Lam. http://home.ust.hk/~lblkt/xml/opac.html and http://home.ust.hk/~lblkt/xml/opac2.html

OPAC Display of a Sample Bibliographic Record in XML Format (without the Chinese Characters)

Record Number	2127507
008 Data	920811s1991||||ch||||||b||||000|0|chi|d
ISBN	9571502537 (deluxe ed.)
ISBN	9571502545 (pbk.)
Catalogin Source	GZM GZM HNK
Call Number	PL2470.Z6 C467 1991
Author	Cheng, Yuan-min.
Title	Chun chiu Tso shih ching chuan chi chieh hsu shu cheng / Cheng Yuan-min chu.
Edition	Chu pan.
Imprint	Tai-pei shih : Tai-wan hsueh sheng shu chu, Min kuo 80 [1991]
Physical Description	112 p. ; 22 cm.
Note	Includes bibliographical references (p. 109-112)
Subject	Confucius. Chun chiu.
Subject	Tso-chiu, Ming. Tso chuan.
Other Author	Tso-chiu, Ming. Tso chuan. 1991.
Other Author	Confucius. Chun chiu. 1991.

OPAC Display of a Sample Bibliographic Record in XML Format (with the Chinese Characters)

Record Number	2127507
008 Data	920811s1991||||ch||||||b||||000|0|chi|d
ISBN	9571502537 (deluxe ed.)
ISBN	9571502545 (pbk.)
Catalogin Source	GZM GZM HNK
Call Number	PL2470.Z6 C467 1991
Author	程元敏.
Author	Cheng, Yuan-min.
Title	春秋左氏經傳集解序疏證 / 程元敏著.
Title	Chun chiu Tso shih ching chuan chi chieh hsu shu cheng / Cheng Yuan-min chu.
Edition	初版.
Edition	Chu pan.
Imprint	臺北市 : 臺灣學生書局, 民國80 [1991]
Imprint	Tai-pei shih : Tai-wan hsueh sheng shu chu, Min kuo 80 [1991]
Physical Description	112 p. ; 22 cm.
Note	Includes bibliographical references (p. 109-112)
Subject	孔子. 春秋.
Subject	Confucius. Chun chiu.
Subject	左丘明. 左傳.
Subject	Tso-chiu, Ming. Tso chuan.
Other Author	左丘明. 左傳. 1991.
Other Author	Tso-chiu, Ming. Tso chuan. 1991.
Other Author	孔子. 春秋. 1991.
Other Author	Confucius. Chun chiu. 1991.

Appendix 3

USMARC Record Converted From XML

Appendix 4 shows how the bibliographic data in Appendix 1 might be encoded in XML.

This example shows how the same record might look in USMARC format converted from XML. The first instance shows the bibliographic record without the Chinese characters. The second instance displays the same record but with the Chinese characters encoded in BIG5 instead of the default encoding scheme, Unicode (UTF-8). An XML-aware browser, like Internet Explorer 5, will understand both of these encoding schemes and display non-roman characters in proper fashion.

Coded by K. T. Lam. http://home.ust.hk/~lblkt/xml/marc2.html and http://home.ust.hk/~lblkt/xml/marc.html.

Sample USMARC Record Converted from XML (without the Chinese Characters)

Leader 06-07: am
001 2127507
008 920811s1991||||ch||||||b||||000|0|chi|d
020 bb |a 9571502537 (deluxe ed.)
020 bb |a 9571502545 (pbk.)
040 bb |a GZM |c GZM |d HNK
090 bb |a PL2470.Z6 |b C467 1991
100 1b |a Cheng, Yuan-min.
245 10 |a Chun chiu Tso shih ching chuan chi chieh hsu shu cheng / |c Cheng Yuan-min chu.
250 bb |a Chu pan.
260 bb |a Tai-pei shih : |b Tai-wan hsueh sheng shu chu, |c Min kuo 80 [1991]
300 bb |a 112 p. ; |c 22 cm.
504 bb |a Includes bibliographical references (p. 109-112)
600 00 |a Confucius. |t Chun chiu.
600 20 |a Tso-chiu, Ming. |t Tso chuan.
700 22 |a Tso-chiu, Ming. |t Tso chuan. |f 1991.
700 02 |a Confucius. |t Chun chiu. |f 1991.

Sample USMARC Record Converted from XML (with the Chinese Characters)

Leader 06-07: am
001 2127507
008 920811s1991||||ch||||||b||||000|0|chi|d
020 bb |a 9571502537 (deluxe ed.)
020 bb |a 9571502545 (pbk.)
040 bb |a GZM |c GZM |d HNK
090 bb |a PL2470.Z6 |b C467 1991
100 1b |a 程元敏.
100 1b |a Cheng, Yuan-min.
245 10 |a 春秋左氏經傳集解序疏證 / |c 程元敏著.
245 10 |a Chun chiu Tso shih ching chuan chi chieh hsu shu cheng / |c Cheng Yuan-min chu.
250 bb |a 初版.
250 bb |a Chu pan.
260 bb |a 臺北市 : |b 臺灣學生書局, |c 民國80 [1991]
260 bb |a Tai-pei shih : |b Tai-wan hsueh sheng shu chu, |c Min kuo 80 [1991]
300 bb |a 112 p. ; |c 22 cm.
504 bb |a Includes bibliographical references (p. 109-112)
600 00 |a 孔子. |t 春秋.
600 00 |a Confucius. |t Chun chiu.
600 20 |a 左丘明. |t 左傳.
600 20 |a Tso-chiu, Ming. |t Tso chuan.
700 22 |a 左丘明. |t 左傳. |f 1991.
700 22 |a Tso-chiu, Ming. |t Tso chuan. |f 1991.
700 02 |a 孔子. |t 春秋. |f 1991.
700 02 |a Confucius. |t Chun chiu. |f 1991.

Appendix 4

XML Format for Bibliographic Data

This example expresses the bibliographic data in Appendix 1 in XML format rather than in SGML. It uses BIG5 to code the Chinese characters instead of the default encoding scheme, Unicode (UTF-8). An XML-aware browser, like Internet Explorer 5, will understand both of these encoding schemes and display non-roman characters in proper fashion.

The example also includes an XSL style sheet for displaying the MARC tags.

Coded by K. T. Lam. See Moving from MARC to XML. http://home.ust.hk/~lblkt/xml/marc2xml.html

XML Format for Bibliographic Data

```
<?xml version="1.0" encoding="big5"?>
<?xml-stylesheet type="text/xsl" href="marc.xsl"?>
<records xmlns:dt="urn:schemas-microsoft-com:datatypes" xml:space="preserve">

  <marc mattype="am" cdate="19980625" udate="19980625" rcn="ABrE">

  <fd name="001" ind1="" ind2="" label="Record Number">
    <sf name="">2127507</sf></fd>

  <fd name="008"  ind1="" ind2="" label="008 Data">
    <sf name="">920811s1991||||ch|||||||b||||000|0|chi|d</sf></fd>

  <fd name="020" ind1="b" ind2="b" label="ISBN">
    <sf name="a">9571502537 (deluxe ed.)</sf></fd>

  <fd name="020" ind1="b" ind2="b" label="ISBN">
    <sf name="a">9571502545 (pbk.)</sf></fd>

  <fd name="040" ind1="b" ind2="b" label="Catalogin Source">
    <sf name="a">GZM</sf>
    <sf name="c">GZM</sf>
    <sf name="d">HNK</sf></fd>

  <fd name="090" ind1="b" ind2="b" label="Call Number">
    <sf name="a">PL2470.Z6</sf>
    <sf name="b">C467 1991</sf></fd>

  <fd name="100" ind1="1" ind2="b" label="Author">
    <sf name="a">程元敏.</sf></fd>

  <fd name="100" ind1="1" ind2="b" label="Author">
    <sf name="a">Cheng, Yuan-min.</sf></fd>

  <fd name="245" ind1="1" ind2="0" label="Title">
    <sf name="a">春秋左氏經傳集解序疏證 /</sf>
    <sf name="c">程元敏著.</sf></fd>

  <fd name="245" ind1="1" ind2="0" label="Title">
    <sf name="a">Chun chiu Tso shih ching chuan chi chieh hsu shu
              cheng /</sf>
    <sf name="c">Cheng Yuan-min chu.</sf></fd>

  <fd name="250" ind1="b" ind2="b" label="Edition">
    <sf name="a">初版.</sf></fd>
```

```
<fd name="250" ind1="b" ind2="b" label="Edition">
  <sf name="a">Chu pan.</sf></fd>

<fd name="260" ind1="b" ind2="b" label="Imprint">
  <sf name="a">臺北市 :</sf>
  <sf name="b">臺灣學生書局,</sf>
  <sf name="c">民國80 [1991]</sf></fd>

<fd name="260" ind1="b" ind2="b" label="Imprint">
  <sf name="a">Tai-pei shih :</sf>
  <sf name="b">Tai-wan hsueh sheng shu chu,</sf>
  <sf name="c">Min kuo 80 [1991]</sf></fd>

<fd name="300" ind1="b" ind2="b" label="Physical Description">
  <sf name="a">112 p. ;</sf>
  <sf name="c">22 cm.</sf></fd>

<fd name="504" ind1="b" ind2="b" label="Note">
  <sf name="a">Includes bibliographical references (p.
             109-112)</sf></fd>

<fd name="600" ind1="0" ind2="0" label="Subject">
  <sf name="a">孔子.</sf>
  <sf name="t">春秋.</sf></fd>

<fd name="600" ind1="0" ind2="0" label="Subject">
  <sf name="a">Confucius.</sf>
  <sf name="t">Chun chiu.</sf></fd>

<fd name="600" ind1="2" ind2="0" label="Subject">
  <sf name="a">左丘明.</sf>
  <sf name="t">左傳.</sf></fd>

<fd name="600" ind1="2" ind2="0" label="Subject">
  <sf name="a">Tso-chiu, Ming.</sf>
  <sf name="t">Tso chuan.</sf></fd>

<fd name="700" ind1="2" ind2="2" label="Other Author">
  <sf name="a">左丘明.</sf>
  <sf name="t">左傳.</sf>
  <sf name="f">1991.</sf></fd>

<fd name="700" ind1="2" ind2="2" label="Other Author">
  <sf name="a">Tso-chiu, Ming.</sf>
  <sf name="t">Tso chuan.</sf>
  <sf name="f">1991.</sf></fd>

<fd name="700" ind1="0" ind2="2" label="Other Author">
  <sf name="a">孔子.</sf>
  <sf name="t">春秋.</sf>
```

```
    <sf name="f">1991.</sf></fd>

  <fd name="700" indl="0" ind2="2" label="Other Author">
    <sf name="a">Confucius.</sf>
    <sf name="t">Chun chiu.</sf>
    <sf name="f">1991.</sf></fd>

</marc>
</records>
```

XSL Stylesheet for Displaying MARC Tags

```
<?xml version='1.0'?>
<xsl:stylesheet xmlns:xsl="http://www.w3.org/TR/WD-xsl">
  <xsl:template match="/">
    <HTML>
      <HEAD>
        <TITLE>Sample Record - XML to MARC</TITLE>
      </HEAD>
      <BODY>
        <H3>Sample USMARC Record converted from XML</H3>
        <xsl:for-each select="records/marc">
          <BR/>
          Leader 06-07:
          <xsl:value-of select="@mattype"/>

          <xsl:for-each select="fd">
            <BR/>
            <xsl:value-of select="@name"/>
            <xsl:value-of select="@indl"/><xsl:value-of select="@ind2"/>

            <xsl:for-each select="sf">
              |<xsl:value-of select="@name"/><xsl:value-of select="."/>
            </xsl:for-each>
          </xsl:for-each>
        </xsl:for-each>

      </BODY>
    </HTML>
  </xsl:template>
</xsl:stylesheet>
```

Index

1Nine Systems, 127
ABC News, 120
AborText, 38
access, 102
Active Reference Linking, 52
ActiveX, 121
actuate, 70, 71
addressing, 57, 58, 74-76, 82, 86
    absolute, 76, 158
    relative, 58, 76, 77, 81, 170
AdeptEditor, 139, 142, 156
Adobe Acrobat, 51, 52
Adobe GoLive, 140
Adobe Systems Inc., 132, 139, 140
AElfred, 95
Agency-Company Organization for Research and Development, 124, 128
agent, 121, 127, 132, 158
Allaire Corp., 149-150
Amazon.com, 120
American Bar Association, 134
American National Standards Institute, 114-115
Anbar Abstracts, 52
ancestor, 79, 86, 87, 158
ancestor-or-self, 87
anchor tag, 58, 158
Anderson Unicom Group, 127
annotations, 69
ANSI ASC X12, 116, 119, 122, 128
application development, 138, 142, 143, 148, 151
application integration, 129, 147
ArborText, 51, 139, 150
Ariba Inc., 124, 127, 129, 132, 134, 150
ASCII, 34, 123, 159
ASCII editor, 137
Association of American Publishers, 9
AT&T, 133
ATTLIST, 16, 20
attribute, 44, 49, 50, 60, 63, 67-71, 87, 133, 141, 159
    position, 48
attribute declaration, 19, 20, 66, 97, 159

attribute list declaration, 67, 159
attribute types, 20
attributes, 11, 19, 33, 45, 56, 61, 64, 65, 79, 81, 83, 97, 104, 118, 123, 148, 149
    remapping, 56
aural style sheet, 52, 54
authentication, 99, 134
authority control, 4
Automotive Network Exchange, 132
axes, 86
axis-name, 83
bar code, 123
bar coding, 127
Barnes & Noble Inc., 120, 130
Barnesandnoble.com, 120, 127
BASIC, 48
Bean Markup Language (BML), 146
behavior, 70, 71, 108
Bertelsmann, 120
Best Buy Co. Inc., 130
binary code, 98
binary data, 28
binary entity, 159
Bioinformatic Sequence Markup Language, 100
BizConnect, 113
BizConnect Author, 113
BizTalk, 130-132
BizTalk Framework, 129-131
BizTalk Repository, 130
BizTalk Steering Committee, 131
BizTalk.org, 129-131
BladeRunner, 139-141
Bluestone Software, 133, 144, 145
Book Data Limited, 128
Book Industry Study Group, Inc., 115, 128
Book Industry Systems Advisory Committee (BISAC), 115, 128
Book Place, 128
book sales, 120
bookmarks, 90
booleans, 57, 82
braille, 32
branches, 94
Bristol-Myers Squibb Co., 127
BT Office Products International, 127
Business Framework and Business Applications Programming Interface, 131
business processes, 114, 125-127, 129, 130

business-to-business, 114-116, 118, 127, 132, 134
BuySite, 131
C++, 95, 97, 150
calculations, 91
Cambridge Scientific Abstracts, 52
CAP, 127
caption, 59, 69
cascade, 35, 36, 159
Cascading Style Sheets (CSS), 31, 34, 38-40, 42, 47, 51, 92, 97, 98, 139, 143, 159
case sensitivity, 12, 77, 137
catalog file, 102, 109, 110
CatchWord, 51, 52
CDATA, 16, 20, 39, 159
Channel Definition Format, 99
Channelware Inc., 132
character data, 24, 111
character entities, 23, 24, 160
character reference, 12, 83, 160
character set, 15
character string, 57, 74, 80
Chemdex Corporation, 127
Chemical Markup Language, 99
Chevron Corp., 127
child elements, 63, 66, 72, 78, 79, 83, 86, 87, 103, 104, 160, 168
Chrystal, 97
Cisco, 127
Claris Corp., 130
CNET Inc., 132
COBOL, 148
ColdFusion, 150
ColdFusion® Web Application Server, 149
Collabria, 127
comments, 12, 14, 15, 69, 81, 86 , 97, 116, 148, 160
    HTML, 15
commerce, 120
Commerce One Inc., 124, 125, 129, 130, 131, 132, 150, 151
CommerceNet, 120, 124, 128, 132
CommerceXML, 124, 127
Common Business Libraries, 132, 151
common catalog format, 110
Common Information Model, 112
CommunityWare/XML Publisher, 140
Compaq, 53
Component Object Model (COM), 131, 139

Compucom, 127
ComputerLiteracy.com, 127
Concur Technologies Inc., 130
configuration file, 109
construction rule, 44-47, 50, 51, 160
consumer, 118, 120, 134
consumer to business, 115
consumer to consumer, 115
content creation, 143
content development, 138, 142
content management, 107, 108, 141, 149
Content Management Suite, 149
content model, 160
content-identifier, 161
content-role, 68, 69, 71
content-title, 69, 71
cookies, 32
copyright, 70
core flow objects, 42, 161
Cort Furniture Rental, 127
cursor property, 37
customized display, 90, 148
cXML, 132, 150
data definition markup language (DDML), 145
data dictionaries, 119, 126, 128
data exchange, 130
data formats, 113
data integrity, 99, 134
data interchange, 95, 112, 115, 121, 147
Data Interchange Standards Association, 5
data manipulation, 141
data mapping, 119
data model, 161
data objects, 132, 145
data processing, viii
Data Research Associates, 8
data sharing, 112, 114, 117, 121-123, 130
database, 4, 82, 91, 92, 103, 123, 133, 138, 139, 144, 145, 147, 148
    flat-file, 103
    object, 104, 141, 148
    object-relational, 104, 106, 150
    relational, 103, 104, 117, 131, 141, 150
database managers, 92
database object browser, 145
DataBots, 121

DataChannel Inc., 95, 97, 125, 130, 131
Datalogic, 139
Dell Computer Corp., 128, 130
descendant, 78, 86, 158, 161
descendant-or-self, 86
Desktop Management Task Force, 112
desktop publishing systems, 13
Development Markup Language, 99
DHTML, 8, 90
Digital Object Identifier, 10
Digital Signature (DSig), 99, 134
Digital Signature Guidelines, 134
digital signatures, 133
display, 69, 141
distributed processing, 122
DOCTYPE, 16
document content definitions (DCDs), 145
Document Content Descriptions (DCD), 5
document declaration, 27
document entity, 23
document fragments, 57, 70
document management, 102
document management systems, 104-107, 139
Document Object Model (DOM), ix, x, 89, 94, 96-98, 121, 139, 142, 147, 148, 161
document storage, 110
Document Style Semantics and Specification Language (DSSSL), 31, 33, 34, 38-42, 45, 161
document type declaration, 16, 22, 161
document type definition see DTD
Documentum, 125
DOM see Document Object Model
DSSSL see Document Style Semantics and Specification Language
DTD, 1, 3, 5-7, 12, 14, 15, 16, 17, 24, 28, 29, 32, 60, 65, 67, 70, 96, 97, 100, 106, 109, 111, 119, 121, 123, 125, 127, 132, 139, 140, 142-146, 149-151, 162
Dublin Core, 8
DXP, 95
Dynamic HTML see DHTML
Dynamic XML with Java, 146
e-business, 115, 129
e-commerce, 121, 127, 130, 132, 134, 135, 147, 149-151
EcmaScript, 47, 50, 97
Eddie Bauer Inc., 130
EDI, 8, 114-118, 121, 122, 127, 128, 162

Edifecs Commerce, 128
EDItEUR, 119, 124, 128
editorial system, 107
electronic business interfaces, 123
electronic commerce,viii, 8, 98, 114, 115, 119, 124, 125, 140, 162
Electronic Data Interchange see EDI
electronic forms, 114, 116, 121, 133, 140
element, 6, 7, 11-14, 16-18, 39, 40, 44, 45, 57, 58, 67, 68, 70, 73, 74, 79, 81, 86, 92, 97, 105, 123, 133, 140, 143 162
    child, 41, 45
    container, 18
    groups, 18
    parameter, 17, 23, 24, 97, 168
    parent, 41, 71, 78, 79, 86, 87, 103, 168
    position, 48
    simple, 171
element content model, 11, 17, 18
element declarations, 20
element occurrence indicator, 18
element tags, 13
element trees, 46
element type declaration, 17
embedded style sheet, 36, 37
Emercis Corp., 130
Encoded Archival Description, 8
encoding declaration, 14
ENCompass, 8
encryption, 134
Endeavor Corp., 8
enterprise resource planning, 132, 148
entity, 11, 12, 16, 21, 22, 102, 105, 108, 109, 110, 111, 162
    external, 23, 24, 26-28, 109, 163
    general, 23-26
    internal, 23, 26, 28
entity declaration, 22, 58, 96, 162
entity manager, 96, 108, 109
entity name, 110
entity reference, 12, 163
Entrust, 134
Enumerated attributes, 21
eXcelon, 148-149
ExLibris, 8
expression, 82-83
extended link group, 56, 64, 66, 71-73, 163
Extensibility Inc., 145

eXtensible Forms Description Language (XFDL), 133
Extensible HTML, 143
external entity declarations, 109
Extricity, 127
field identifiers, 116
file conversion, 101
file-to-file linking, 102
Fireworks, 140
flow object, 41, 42, 45, 51, 163
flow object tree, 41, 46
following, 78, 79, 87
following-sibling, 87
Ford Motor Co., 128
foreign characters, 4
formatter, 43
formatting object, 46
formatting objects, 42
Formatting Output Specification Instance (FOSI), 33
formatting semantics, 43
forms processing, 133
fragment identifier, 57, 67, 75-77, 86
fragments, 70, 73
frame, 60
FrameLink, 139
FrameMaker, 140
FrameMaker+SGML, 139, 150
FrontPage 2000, 140
fsibling, 78, 79
ftp, 58, 121, 130
General Motors Corp., 131
gopher, 58
Graphic Communications Association, 5, 125
graphics, 21, 69, 71, 98, 140
grove, 94, 163
Guideline XML, 128
handheld device, 133
Handheld Device Markup Language, 99
Harbinger Corp., 127, 130
header, 58
Health Level 7, 100, 124
here, 78
hierarchical data, 112
hierarchical data structures, 96, 103
Hollinger International Inc., 132
HoTMetaL, 138

HP-UX, 150
HTML, viii, 1, 2, 8-10, 12, 14, 31, 33-37, 39, 40, 42, 51, 53, 56-60, 62, 66-69, 72, 74, 75, 81, 88-90, 96-98, 105, 112, 120, 122, 127-129, 133, 137, 138, 140, 142, 147, 151, 164
HTML anchor, 75
HTML+TIME, 53
HTTP, 27, 58, 112, 121, 130, 144
hyperlink see also link, tag, metatag, 23, 56, 80, 81
Hypertext, viii, 164
HyTime, 60, 164
IBM, 5, 53, 97, 106, 125, 128, 130, 131, 142, 144, 146, 147
Icon Information-Systems, 142
ID attribute, 21, 39, 47, 57, 74-77, 79, 81, 86
identifier, 67
identifier type, 111
IDREF, 21
IGNORE, 16
INCLUDE, 16
incompatible formats, 101
Information and Content Exchange, 132
Informix, 106, 150
inline, 71
inline styles, 37, 50
Inso Corporation, 38
The Internet Society, 118
integrity checker, 96
intellectual property rights, 100
Intelligent software agents, 100
Interactive Pointers, 80
Interchange 2000, 132
Interleaf, 139, 140
International Data Corp., 120
Internet Engineering Task Force (IETF), 118
Internet Explorer, 6, 43, 51, 52, 97, 132, 143, 146
Internet Open Trading Protocol, 98
Interoperability, 90, 100
InterWorld, 127
intranet, 105, 121
inverted word index, 105
IPNet Solutions, 140
Ironside, 127
J.D. Edwards & Co., 130
ISBN, 4, 8, 91, 92, 128
Java, 51, 75, 95, 97, 100, 121, 133, 142-144, 146-148, 150, 165
Java applet, 8, 29, 32, 98

Java Development Kit, 142
Java Messaging Service, 144
Java Speech Markup Language, 99
Java Virtual Machine, 51
JavaBeans, 146, 147
JavaScript, 47, 50, 98
JetForm Corp., 133
John Wiley & Sons, 9
Johnson & Johnson, 128
Kmart, 117
knowledge management, 107, 115, 148
Lark, 95
Level 8 Systems, 130
Library of Congress, 3
Life Technologies, 127
link, 57, 60, 68, 69, 81, 115, 128, 139, 141, 165
    bi-directional, 72
    extended, 56, 60-63, 66-68, 163
    HTML, 58
    inline, 60-62
    multidirectional, 60, 72, 73
    out-of-line, 60, 61, 64, 65, 78, 168
    relative, 26, 78, 170
    simple, 56, 60, 61, 62, 63, 69, 75, 171
    typed, 57, 60
    XML, 59
Link element, 36, 54
link loops, 73
link rot, 52, 62
linked style sheet, 36, 37
linking, 56, 57, 103, 108
linking element, 59, 60-62, 66, 69, 133, 165
linking resource, 69, 71
Linux, 142
LISP, 38
location path, 83
    absolute, 85, 86
    relative, 85, 86
location steps, 85, 86
locator, 59, 60-62, 66, 70-72, 74, 76, 78, 103, 165
Lockheed Martin Corp., 128
logical markup, 81
logical structure, 6, 7, 11, 13, 16, 22, 82, 165
Logos Research Systems, Inc., 5
Lotus Notes, 140

LotusXSL, 95
Lucent Technologies, 133
macro, 13, 47, 50, 51, 139, 165
Macromedia, 53, 140
mail merge, 82
mailto, 58
mapping, 117, 146
MARC, 3, 4, 8
MARC format, 94, 119
MARC record, vii, 5, 7
MARCType Parser, 5
MARCXML, 5
Marimba, 98
MarketSite, 131, 151
markup see also tag, metatag, 12, 13, 19, 29, 32, 33, 35, 40, 47, 74, 81, 92, 93, 97, 123, 166
markup attributes, 32
markup declaration, 166
markup language, vii, viii, 16, 56
MasterCard International, Inc., 128
Mathematics Markup Language, 100
McGraw-Hill Construction Information Group, 127
message queuing, 130
metadata, vii, 5, 19, 100, 103, 141, 166
Metadata Information Clearing House (Interactive) – MICI, 9, 10
metalanguage, vii, 10, 166
metatag see also markup, tag, 6, 115, 118-120, 128, 149
Microsoft Access, 146
Microsoft Corp., 5, 38, 43, 51-53, 90, 95, 98, 124, 128-132, 134, 140, 143, 146, 148
Microsoft Message Queue Server, 130
Microsoft Transaction Server, 148
Microsoft Word, 139, 140
Microstar Software, 95, 140, 142
MIME, 29, 39, 74, 166
mobile telephones, 99
Motorola, 53, 133
MQSeries, 130, 144
MSXML, 95
multimedia, 29, 54, 59, 62, 69, 99, 120, 149
Multipurpose Internet Mail Extension see MIME
NAME, 76
namespace, ix, 6, 43, 83, 125, 143, 146, 167
National Semiconductor Corp., 132
natural language, 103

navigation, 72, 86, 99
NCR Systemedia Group, 127
Near & Far Designer, 3, 138, 142
nest, 19, 41, 50, 73, 94, 96, 105
Netscape Communications Corp., 90, 97, 128
Netscape Navigator, 6, 132
news, 58
News Internet Services, 132
NICEM, 9
NMTOKEN, 21
nntp, 58
node, 57, 74, 77, 78, 82, 83, 85-87, 94, 167
non-repudiability, 99, 134
normalization, 167
NOTATION, 16, 30, 34, 58, 75, 97, 111, 167
notations, 11, 28, 29
OASIS, 124, 129
OASIS Registry and Repository Technical Committee, 125
OBI, 124, 128
Object Design Inc., 147-148
Object Management Group Inc., 124
object linking and embedding, 108
object-oriented programming, 96
object-oriented software, 104
OCLC, 8, 52
ODBC, 140
OECD, 99
Office Depot, 127
Online catalogs, 120, 131
Open Applications Group Inc., 124
Open Buying on the Internet see OBI
Open Financial Exchange Specification, 98
Open Tag, 99
Oracle Corp., 95, 97, 106, 125, 147
Organization for the Advancement of Structured Information Standards see OASIS
origin, 78
out-of-line, 167
overhead projector, 32
owner identifier, 111
palm computers, 99, 133
parent see entity, parent
parse, 92, 106
parsed entity, 24, 28
parser, 2, 5, 19, 28, 76, 80, 82, 89, 95, 96, 133, 142, 143, 147, 151, 168

Java, 6
non-validating, 6
validating, 6
Partner Interface Process, 125, 126
pattern, 45-47, 49, 168
PCDATA (parsed character data), 19
PDF, 51, 52, 74, 140
PenOp, 134
PeopleSoft, 130
Perl, 97
personalization, 108, 148, 149
physical markup, 82
Physical separation, 35
physical structure, 11, 22, 168
PICS (Platform for Internet Content Selection), 134, 169
Platform for Privacy Preferences, 98
POET Software, 97, 127, 147, 14 9, 150
pointer, 16, 104, 109
portable interchange format, 90
Postscript, 51, 140
preceding, 78, 79, 86, 87
preceding-sibling, 87
predicate, 83, 86
Pretty Good Privacy, 98
Preview Travel Inc., 132
privacy, 98, 100
processing, 89, 100, 121, 139
conditional, 48
direct, 48
event-driven, 93
out-of-sequence, 93
restricted, 48
tree-manipulation, 93
processing instruction, 12, 14, 15, 39, 50, 77, 81, 86, 97, 169
processor, 2, 15, 19, 25, 27, 43, 48-51, 75, 76, 83, 92, 93, 96, 174
style sheet, 42
prolog, 14, 15, 169
prospero, 58
protocol, 58, 99, 113, 115, 121, 125, 130, 132, 144
psibling, 78, 79
public identifier, 26, 27, 29, 30, 102, 108, 110
public key encryption, 98
public text class, 111
Push Media, 99
Python, 95

QuickTime, 29, 76
Real Audio, 16
RealPage, 52
recommendation, viii, ix, x, 1, 34, 38, 39, 54, 96, 97, 118, 123, 134
remapping, 71
remote data file, 111
repository, 104, 124, 125, 129, 130, 132, 140, 141, 148, 149
reserved attributes, 22
reserved name indicator, 19
resource, 59, 61, 62, 66, 68, 72, 73, 75-78, 81, 86
    inline, 67
    local, 59, 63, 64, 66-68
    out-of-line, 67
    remote, 59, 63, 64, 66, 67, 68, 69, 70, 72
    target, 67
Resource Description Framework, ix, 5, 98, 100, 170
responsibility element, 18
result tree, 43, 45
RightDoc, 139
Rockefeller Foundation, 99
role, 67, 71
romanization, 4
root rule, 46
RosettaNet, 124, 125
RoweCom, 127
SAP AG, 125, 130, 131
Sapphire/Web, 144
Saqqara Systems, 127
SAX, 89, 94, 95, 96, 142, 147, 151, 170
Schema, x, 3, 4, 5, 91, 112, 123-125, 129-132, 134, 138, 145, 146, 149, 150, 151, 170
schemas for object-oriented XML (SOX), 145
Scriptics Corp., 112
scripting, 133, 170
scripts, 50, 90, 96, 122
search engine, vii, 4, 10, 68, 100, 103, 105,106, 120, 123
    Aleph, 8
Secure Sockets Layer, 144
security, 98, 134
self, 87
semantics, 40, 57, 61, 62, 74, 111, 124, 128,131, 134
Sequoia Software, 132
SGML, vii, viii, 1-4, 6, 7, 12, 29-31, 34, 52, 56, 59, 67, 104, 106, 111, 137-139, 149, 150, 171
SGML Open, 110

Sharp Electronics Corp., 130
show, 69-71, 75
sibling, 79
sibling elements, 171
siblings, 48, 94, 103
signature, x, 99
Signed Document Markup Language, 98
Silanis, 134
Silfide, 95
SilverPlatter, 52
Simple API for XML see SAX
SiteSearch, 7
smart data, 112
SMIL (Synchronized Multimedia Integration Language), ix, 53, 54, 171
SMTP, 121
SoftQuad, 125, 138, 139, 150
Solaris, 142, 150
sorting, 49
source, 59, 70
specification, viii, ix, 34, 36, 38, 54, 56, 57, 69, 78, 97, 112, 121, 130, 131, 139, 145
Speech Markup Language, 53
speech synthesizer, 43, 99
speech-to-text converter, 53
SpeechML, 53
spreadsheet, 92, 112, 148
SQL, 99, 103, 144, 145, 147
standard, viii, ix, 67, 93, 114, 116, 118, 119, 124, 128, 130, 134, 135
Staples, 127
steps, 71, 73
Sterling Commerce, 127, 130
Stilo Technology, Ltd., 139, 141
streaming media, 76
string attribute, 20
string matching, 74, 80
string-matching, 77
strings, 57, 82
structured communications, 115
structured data, 92, 120
style language, 31, 34, 38
style rule, 44, 46, 47, 50
style sheet, ix, 13, 32, 33, 36, 40, 42-45, 51, 97, 106, 108, 139, 141, 150, 171
Stylus, 51
Sun Microsystems Inc., 51, 95, 97, 125, 132
SXP, 95

Syntactical separation, 35
syntax, 3, 4, 6, 10, 16, 20, 38, 40, 57, 62, 74-76, 78, 82, 83, 99, 110, 117, 129, 134, 138, 139, 143, 145, 172
synthesized speech, 99
system identifier, 27, 30, 109, 110
tables, 34, 41, 48, 92, 103, 104, 141, 145
tag see also markup, metatag, 2, 5, 6, 7, 10-14, 16, 19, 21, 32, 33, 36, 37, 45, 46, 47, 66, 75, 76, 90, 92, 96, 99, 118, 123-125, 128, 129, 137, 172
target, 59, 69, 70, 172
Tcl, 113
TEI see Text Encoding Initiative
telnet, 58
template, 17, 42, 43, 45, 119, 122, 131, 140, 150
TeX, 100, 146
Texcel, 97
TeXML, 146
TEXT, 111
Text Encoding Initiative, 8, 60, 172
text-to-speech conversion, 53-54
Timed Interactive Multimedia Extensions, 53
title, 59, 64, 68, 69, 71, 128
Tokenized attributes, 21
tokens, 13
transactional data, 123
transform, 43
Transformis, 51
transition effects, 71
Translation Memory Exchange, 99
Transportation Data Coordinating Committee, 114
traversal, 57, 59, 60, 69, 70, 74, 76, 78, 172
tree, 74, 82, 83, 86, 92, 94, 140, 143, 145, 147, 172
tree transformation, 43
Tribune Media Services, 132
typesetting tags, 13
UN/EDIFACT, 116, 119, 121, 122, 128
UNESCO, 99
Unicode, 24
Uniform Resource Identifier, 7, 16, 27
Uniform Resource Identifier Reference, 74
Unisoft Wares, 133
Universal Listener Framework (ULF), 144
unparsed data, 21
unparsed entities, 24
US Technologies, 127

USMARC, 3-5
valid document, 65, 173
validating parser, 6, 173
validation, 129, 130, 140, 143, 151
validity, 3, 6, 142
value added network, 121
VBScript, 97
Veo Systems Inc., 132
verification, 134
VeriSign, 134
version control, 106, 141
Vervet Logic, 139, 141
Vignette Corp., 127, 132
virtual documents, 69
Virtual Reality Modeling Language, 99
Visual XML, 99, 133, 143-146
Vitria Technology Inc., 130
voice browser, 53
Voice Markup Language, 53
VoxML, 53
VXML, 133
W3C, vii-x, 5, 7, 34, 38, 39, 52-54, 94, 97, 121, 123, 131, 133, 134, 139, 142, 145, 173
wais, 58
Wal-Mart, 117
Web Methods, 127, 130
Web of Science, 52
Webb Interactive Services, 140
WebBroker, 98
WebWriter, 139, 141
well-formed, 6, 7, 14, 173
white space, 12, 13, 22, 92, 171, 173
WHO, 99
Windows, 142, 143, 150
Windows NT, 140, 148, 150
wizard, 144
WML, 132
World Wide Web Committee see W3C
WordPerfect, 137
work-arounds, ix, 51, 102
World Bank, 99
WXML, 132, 133
WYSIWYG, 11, 137, 139, 140, 142
X12, 114, 116
XCAT Project, 128

XHTML, 143
Xlink, x, 38, 56-58, 60-62, 64, 65, 67, 69-71, 73, 74, 78, 81, 87, 88
XLL, 54, 56, 57, 173
XmetaL, 138, 139, 141-143, 150
XML authoring tool, 81
XML Authority, 145, 146
XML Bean Maker, 146
XML declaration, 14
XML Development Kit, 150, 151
XML for Java, 95
XML Forms Architecture (XFA), 133
XML Library, 95
XML Linking Language see XLL
XML Namespaces see namespaces
XML Parser for Java, 147
XML Pro, 139, 141-143
XML processor see processor
XML Productivity Kit for Java, 147
XML Query Language see XQL
XML Schema see also schema, x, 131
XML Spy, 142, 143, 146
XML Styler, 51, 52
XML Working Group, vii
xml.org, 124
xml:lang, 22
xml:link, 66
xml:space, 22
XML-Data, 145, 146
XML-Signature Requirements, 98
XP, 95
Xpath, x, 56-58, 74, 76, 82, 83, 86, 88
Xpointer, x, 6, 56, 57, 59, 67, 73-78, 80-82, 87, 88, 174
XQL, 99, 148
XQL Query Wizard, 149
XSL, x, 8, 31, 38, 40, 42, 46, 50, 58, 74, 87, 91, 121, 132, 140, 141, 143, 149, 174
XSL processor, 147
XSL template, 92
XSL Transformations (XSLT), x, 40, 57, 82
Z39.50, 4
ZDNet, 132
zero install software, 98
Zona Research Inc., 120